"Here's what I like about this book: two stories intertwine—the author's story of her relationship with the Savior and how He brought her to freedom in Himself *and* the Savior's story of His incomparable attributes as He manifests them repeatedly in Lisa's life. By inference, we who know Christ personally have that same opportunity and privilege of seeing these attributes at work in our own lives. Lisa reminds us to stop, take notice, and give thanks for the fact that the Son has set us free so we are free indeed. Now, all we have to do is believe it…and enjoy it."

—LUCI SWINDOLL, Women of Faith speaker and author

"Lisa Harper knocks me out! *Untamed* invites me to experience the wild side of Jesus without losing the gentle side of Jesus. The book's wonderfully balanced perspective motivates me to pursue Him with new vigor."

—MARILYN MEBERG, Women of Faith speaker and author of *Tell Me Everything*

"Rarely does a book merit the descriptions 'transformative' and 'mind-altering,' but Lisa Harper earned both with *Untamed*. I was at once unsettled by her challenges to my mental images of Jesus and reminded that, while He walked this earth, He was both completely of this world and wholly otherworldly. Lisa Harper's writing invites you to view Jesus in a dangerously daring and honest way by placing spiritual 3-D glasses on your mind and heart."

—ANITA RENFROE, comedian and author

untamed

How the *Wild* Side of Jesus Frees Us to Live and Love with Abandon

LISA HARPER

AUTHOR OF *A PERFECT MESS*

WATERBROOK
PRESS

UNTAMED
PUBLISHED BY WATERBROOK PRESS
12265 Oracle Boulevard, Suite 200
Colorado Springs, Colorado 80921

All Scripture quotations, unless otherwise indicated, are taken from The Holy Bible, English Standard Version, copyright © 2001 by Crossway Bibles, a division of Good News Publishers. Used by permission. All rights reserved. Scripture quotations marked (MSG) are taken from The Message by Eugene H. Peterson. Copyright © 1993, 1994, 1995, 1996, 2000, 2001, 2002. Used by permission of NavPress Publishing Group. All rights reserved. Scripture quotations marked (NCV) are taken from the New Century Version®. Copyright © 1987, 1988, 1991 by Thomas Nelson Inc. Used by permission. All rights reserved. Scripture quotations marked (NIV) are taken from the Holy Bible, New International Version®. NIV®. Copyright © 1973, 1978, 1984 by International Bible Society. Used by permission of Zondervan Publishing House. All rights reserved. Scripture quotations marked (NLT) are taken from the Holy Bible, New Living Translation, copyright © 1996, 2004. Used by permission of Tyndale House Publishers Inc., Wheaton, Illinois 60189. All rights reserved.

Details in some anecdotes and stories have been changed to protect the identities of the persons involved.

ISBN 978-1-4000-7480-8
ISBN 978-0-307-45907-7 (electronic)

Published in the United States by WaterBrook Multnomah, an imprint of the Crown Publishing Group, a division of Random House Inc., New York.

WATERBROOK and its deer colophon are registered trademarks of Random House Inc.

Library of Congress Cataloging-in-Publication Data
Harper, Lisa, 1963-
    Untamed : how the wild side of Jesus frees us to live and love with abandon / Lisa Harper. — 1st ed.
        p. cm.
    Includes bibliographical references (p.   ).
    ISBN 978-1-4000-7480-8 — ISBN 978-0-307-45907-7 (electronic)
    1. Jesus Christ—Example. I. Title.
    BT304.2.H365 2010
    232.9'04—dc22

                                2010000198

Printed in the United States of America
2010—First Edition

10 9 8 7 6 5 4 3 2 1

SPECIAL SALES
Most WaterBrook Multnomah books are available at special quantity discounts when purchased in bulk by corporations, organizations, and special-interest groups. Custom imprinting or excerpting can also be done to fit special needs. For information, please e-mail SpecialMarkets@WaterBrookMultnomah.com or call 1-800-603-7051.

To my little brother, John Price Angel,
a wild man with a beautiful heart.

Contents

Contents

Introduction

Beauty on the Other Side of the Brink

I love pure speed and pristine mountains, and one of my favorite places to combine the two is Jackson Hole, Wyoming. Jackson Hole is a bit off the beaten path when it comes to snow-skiing resorts, so the town isn't overdeveloped with fast-food restaurants, nor are the slopes jam-packed like a shopping mall on the day after Thanksgiving. It's still a relatively unspoiled Eden, where the local elk population outnumbers the tourists.

One of my favorite ski runs at Jackson Hole is called Timbered Island. Just after you exit the lift, there's a spot so steep it's essentially a cliff face. As a matter of fact, if you stop on the catwalk and turn your skis downhill, the tips will jut out into thin air. However, that alarming pitch levels out into a gently sloped field flanked with towering pine trees. Therefore, if you're daring enough to go over the edge, you're rewarded by the feeling of flying—of weightless freedom—followed by cruising into a soft playground of white crystals. It is absolutely exhilarating! Every time I've gasped in slightly terrified awe at the top, but I've ended up laughing in sheer delight while zooming to the bottom.

Yet despite the spine-tingling payoff, I've noticed that most skiers glide right past the precipice without stopping to consider the view, much less consider jumping off. Perhaps because the trail map designates Timbered Island as a "blue run" (which means the terrain is negotiable for skiers of average skill level), they're seeking a cushy, nonjarring ride. Maybe they've become so accustomed to moderate inclines that they're not even tempted to consider a riskier, more vertical route.

Choosing the safe but boring path is an apt metaphor for the years I spent rather numbly and halfheartedly pursuing God. As Francis Chan candidly describes in his book *Crazy Love,*

> I called myself a Christian, was pretty involved in church, and tried to stay away from all of the things that "good Christians" avoid—drinking, drugs, sex, swearing. Christianity was simple: fight your desires in order to please God. Whenever I failed (which was often), I'd walk around feeling guilty and distant from God.
>
> In hindsight, I don't think my church's teachings were incorrect, just incomplete. My view of God was narrow and small.[1]

Thankfully, I came to a spiritual cliff face that challenged my small, narrow view of God. I got to the edge of who I'd previously understood Jesus to be and risked going beyond it. And the reward has been much more liberating and exhilarating than anything I've ever experienced on skis. Choosing to explore past the boundaries of my incomplete perception has led me to a bigger and better view of our Redeemer. I've discovered Jesus to be much more confrontational and provocative than the pale imitation of Him I had settled for!

As we explore some of His wilder aspects for the next two hundred or so pages together, I really hope you'll get a bigger and better view too. I hope you'll sense the Holy Spirit drawing you into a riskier, more intimate, and less religious relationship with Jesus. I hope that it'll reawaken the sense of adventure God hard-wired into your soul. That you'll find yourself awed by His power and glory and laugh out loud with sheer delight over the fact that this majestically untamed Savior is madly in love with you!

Furthermore, although *Untamed* isn't formatted like a traditional Bible study, I hope it will encourage you to experience Scripture in a fresh way. Each chapter includes an icebreaker question to prompt you to connect your own experience with the topic at hand. At the end of each chapter, you'll also find questions in the "Living and Loving with Abandon" section geared toward helping you reflect on how the "wild side" of Jesus can impact your heart today. These questions are especially stimulating when discussed over coffee with friends!

I believe you'll find *Untamed* to be an interesting book-club selection, an engaging Sunday school curriculum, or even a useful tool to help your women's Bible study group explore the life and ministry of Christ. I sincerely pray it'll help you experience some of the same freedom God has been lavishing on me lately.

Most of all I pray it quickens your heart to wonder and worship over the mind-blowing miracle that King Jesus chooses us as the objects of His affection!

1

Exposing the Myth of a Milquetoast Messiah

Our Savior Is *Wildly* Redemptive

We have very efficiently pared the claws of the
Lion of Judah, certified Him "meek and mild,"
and recommended Him as a fitting household
pet for pale curates and pious old ladies.

—DOROTHY SAYERS

■ ■ ■ ■ ■ ■

B race yourself.

This book is all about getting caught up in a new sense of freedom. In our efforts to achieve maximum buoyancy, along the way we'll be jettisoning a number of mistaken beliefs and a bunch of misplaced guilt.

To start things off, I've decided to clear my conscience of this long-held secret: I used to have a huge crush on Stan Brock. My prepubescent girlfriends nursed crushes on more familiar '60s and '70s icons like Lee Majors, the squinty-eyed actor who starred in the television show *The Six Million Dollar Man,* or rock stars like the plaid-clad Bay City Rollers. But throughout elementary and middle school, I was stuck on Stan, who achieved only marginal fame as Marlin Perkins's sidekick on the NBC series *Mutual of Omaha's Wild Kingdom.*

It didn't matter to me that Stan wasn't a household name or a guitar hero; I thought he was incredibly cool. My heart was his to lose after the episode when he wrestled a giant, angry anaconda into submission. I'd never before seen such courage in the face of danger. Of course he didn't look half bad in his safari outfit either! Genteel, white-haired Marlin had more sound bites, but brave Stan—who lived among the Wapishana Indians in the Central Amazon Basin as a teen—fully captured my attention and affection.

Fate brought him to our small town during the height of the show's popularity and my crush. I can still remember the surge of happiness I felt when the local newspaper announced he was going to be the grand marshal of our Christmas parade. I talked Mom into taking me to the parade early so I could get a front-row seat on the curb. My anticipation built as I waited to see Stan Brock in person. The silly clowns zipping by on tiny scooters held no interest for me. I simply craned my neck, attempting to peer past the marching band and catch the first possible glimpse of my hero as he came into view.

He finally came galloping down First Avenue, riding bareback on a big horse. I think he might've been barefoot too. He had on the same khaki clothes he always wore on the show, and he grinned at me when he rode past. To this day I'm convinced he winked. Right. At. Me! Utterly and completely smitten, I chased after him for a few blocks before reluctantly and dutifully stopping in front of Faust's drugstore so Mom wouldn't worry. In my biased and breathless ten-year-old opinion, Stan was the man!

> Describe the most compelling hero from your childhood. What specific characteristics attracted your admiration?

Now here's a bigger confession: until recently I found Stan a more compelling hero than Jesus in many ways. Don't get me wrong. I loved Jesus wholeheartedly; I just wasn't really sure He was strong enough for me to trust Him with the full weight of my life. In contrast to Stan's strong physique and untamed persona, my mental picture of Jesus sketched a skinny, mild-mannered fellow. Sort of like Clark Kent, only paler.

I attribute that milquetoast image partly to hearing more sermons about Jesus as a carpenter than as a sword-wielding deliverer. It also didn't help to see Him depicted as a sad-eyed blond guy in religious paintings, in which the artists seem to have ignored the fact that Jesus was a Jew who grew up in the Middle East, so He was probably dark headed and olive skinned.

Mostly though, the emasculated Redeemer of my imagination was shaped by my own fear and insecurity. While my girlhood champion had been a risk-taking tough guy, as a grown woman I settled for safe when it came to a Savior. Probably because some of the "tough guys" I'd had relationships with in the past had left bruises. A few bloomed purple on my body, but the most serious wounds were inflicted on my heart, which left me wary. So I edited out the seemingly rough and wild parts of Jesus and squished Him into a box small enough for me to comfortably carry around.

Until one day I finally realized my squashed caricature of Jesus wasn't big enough to calm my anxiety or heal my wounds or defeat the wickedness in our world. Pretending Jesus was less than He actually is resulted in someone I wasn't compelled to worship. So I began a journey to discover the whole Jesus—including the seemingly rough and wild parts—revealed in the Bible. And I found Him to be considerably bigger and better than I ever dreamed possible.

In fact, I discovered that in the very beginning of the Gospels, before our incarnate Savior even appeared on the scene in person, He proved to be *wildly redemptive.*

DON'T SKIP THE BEST PART

Before we go any further, I should probably encourage you to grab a cup of coffee or a Diet Coke, because initially the following passage is going to seem more like a cure for insomnia than a lens through which we'll be able to see Jesus bigger!

> This is the family history of Jesus Christ. He came from the family of David, and David came from the family of Abraham.
>
> Abraham was the father of Isaac.
>
> Isaac was the father of Jacob.
>
> Jacob was the father of Judah and his brothers.
>
> Judah was the father of Perez and Zerah.
>
> (Their mother was *Tamar*.)
>
> Perez was the father of Hezron.
>
> Hezron was the father of Ram.
>
> Ram was the father of Amminadab.
>
> Amminadab was the father of Nahshon.
>
> Nahshon was the father of Salmon.
>
> Salmon was the father of Boaz.
>
> (Boaz's mother was *Rahab*.)
>
> Boaz was the father of Obed.
>
> (Obed's mother was *Ruth*.)
>
> Obed was the father of Jesse.
>
> Jesse was the father of King David.
>
> David was the father of Solomon.
>
> (Solomon's mother had been *Uriah's wife*.)
>
> *Matthew 1:1–6, NCV; emphasis added*

Not exactly riveting reading at first, is it? It's sort of like when someone invites you to view a photo album of their family reunion. However, when you understand the context of Matthew's account of the family tree of Jesus, it gets very interesting.

First of all, Matthew was gabbing to a Jewish audience. And when this gospel was written, women weren't recorded in Jewish genealogies. Although those ancient mamas had their babies without ice chips or epidurals, they were seldom included in official birth records.

■ ■ ■ ■ ■ ■ ■ The *Wild* Ways of God ■ ■ ■ ■ ■ ■

Whereas Matthew traces the genealogy of Jesus back to Abraham, probably to underscore the Messiah's Jewish roots, Luke traces the genealogy of Jesus all the way back to Adam (Luke 3:23–38), probably to prove that Jesus is the hope for *all* mankind, not just the Jews.

There are other significant differences in Matthew's and Luke's genealogy records, most notably naming different fathers for Joseph (Jacob in Matthew 1:16 and Heli in Luke 3:23), which many theologians attribute to Matthew's emphasizing royal succession while Luke emphasized actual physical descent. (Remember, Joseph was technically Jesus's "stepfather," not His biological dad.) There are differing explanations for the naming of two different fathers for Joseph, but the most sensible one is that Joseph's real dad died, and his mom remarried. Thus, Joseph was the physical son of one and the legal son of another.[1]

Therefore, while modern readers are tempted to skip over the beginning of Matthew to get to the good parts where Jesus walks on water or a paralytic turns cartwheels, the original audience for this sermon was probably shocked. They couldn't believe Matthew had the audacity to trample on Jewish propriety. They were probably texting each other messages like *Can you believe this? Matt's including chicks in the genealogy of Immanuel!*

But what I find really interesting is that the women highlighted in these first six verses of Matthew—Tamar, Rahab, Ruth, and Bathsheba—aren't stereotypical Hebrew good girls. Instead, much like you and me, each of them had some ugliness hidden in her past that made it doubtful her name would show up anywhere close to that of the Messiah.

RIPPED FROM THE TABLOIDS

Tamar, the first girl Matthew mentions, was sort of like the Old Testament version of Elizabeth Taylor: she made quite a habit of walking down the aisle! You can find the unabridged version of her story in Genesis 38, but I'll give you the brief edition. Her first husband was the eldest son of a man named Judah, a pretty important guy. Judah was a brother of Joseph, the guy with the multicolored coat. Like each of his brothers, Judah eventually became the father of an entire "tribe," one of twelve people groups that descended from Joseph and his brothers.

Tamar's first hubby, "Judah Jr." (his name was actually Er!), was a stinker, so God killed him. Then Tamar was married to Judah's second eldest son, Onan. Icky though that sounds to our modern ears, the arrangement—called a levirate marriage—was a culturally kosher setup. When a man died without having produced an heir, his brother was to marry the widow and produce a son to carry on the name of husband number one.[2] But Onan was a stinker too, so God killed him.

Next man up to bat was Shelah, Judah's baby boy. But Judah apparently decided he had a "black widow" for a daughter-in-law. Essentially he told her, "Hey, Tamar, since Shelah hasn't gone through puberty yet, why don't you go back home and hang out with your family. I'll call you when he's ready to tango."

This got Tamar scheming for a way to get Judah to live up to his responsibilities sooner rather than later—or likely, never. She ended up disguising herself as a prostitute and lured her father-in-law into sleeping with her. Her dastardly plan succeeded; she wound up pregnant by Judah, her father-in-law. Yuck!

When her condition—and her immorality—became apparent, Judah commanded that Tamar be burned to death, unaware of his role in fathering her unborn twins. Of course, he had a dramatic change of heart when she revealed that she was the "prostitute" he had slept with and declared, "These babies are yours, big boy!"

Tamar was not exactly an ideal candidate for ancestor of the year, but the second girl mentioned in Matthew 1, Rahab, was every bit as scandalous. Rahab's story is found in Joshua 2, and suffice it to say, she didn't have to disguise herself as a prostitute; she was a card-carrying member of the Notorious Ladies of the Evening union! So why was she included in the Messiah's lineage?

IT'S ENOUGH TO MAKE JERRY SPRINGER BLUSH

Right now you're probably wondering how a *good* girl like Ruth—one of only two women to have an entire Old Testament book in her name—ended up in this list of unlikely leading ladies. And I agree with you; as an individual, Ruth was faithful. Her story provides a poignant picture of loyalty and restoration. But if you look up through the branches of her family tree, you'll see that Ruth's heritage goes all the way back to Genesis 19, to the trashy cities of Sodom and Gomorrah.

Sodom and Gomorrah were so wicked—think a double dose of Las Vegas and then some—that God decided to destroy them and all their depraved inhabitants. Except for one fellow named Lot, who loved God. In light of Lot's faithfulness—actually much of the faithfulness credited to him was borrowed from Abraham—God agreed to allow him to escape with his wife and two daughters before He brought the hammer down on Sodom and Gomorrah. But God set one important condition: under no circumstances were they allowed to look back on their way out of town.[3]

Let me assure you that the following commentary can't be found in the Bible; it resides solely in my imagination. But I like to think that Lot and Mrs. Lot had just finished a floor-to-ceiling remodel of their kitchen. Mrs. Lot had fussed and pouted until Lot finally dug deep in his pockets to spring for granite countertops and stainless-steel appliances. It was the kitchen she'd always dreamed of, and the desperate housewives of her cul-de-sac were drooling with envy.

As they were sprinting out of Sodom and Gomorrah, all Mrs. Lot could think was, *I don't want to leave my gorgeous new kitchen!* So she disobeyed God, looked back in greedy longing, and got zapped into a pillar of salt—establishing her place in history as the original "Scary Spice"!

Whatever the reason behind Mrs. Lot's undisciplined eyes, we do know that only Lot and his two girls made it out alive.

The end of Genesis 19 tells us the three of them ended up living in a cave. They'd barely had time to measure for drapes and carpeting when Lot's older daughter turned to the younger one and declared in a huff, "This is a real bummer. There aren't any available bachelors up here. You and I are going to end up lonely old maids if we don't do something about it!"

Obviously, I'm taking just a little bit of liberty with the original Hebrew, but the point is that these girls hatched a plot even more revolting than Tamar's. Lot's daughters got him drunk and both were physically intimate with him on successive nights. Both girls got pregnant, and both had baby boys. The oldest daughter named her son Moab, which translated into English means "from Father."[4] His descendants were known as Moabites, a people group so wicked that God forbade them to enter the Tent of Meeting, the portable temple the Israelites used for worship while they were wandering in the wilderness.[5]

Which brings us back to Ruth, a *Moabite* and the third woman woven into the genealogy of Jesus. Although most of us consider her to be a good girl, based on the book of Ruth, a first-century Jewish audience would surely be thinking, *Yikes, that girl comes from way over on the wrong side of the tracks. Her family tree is rooted in incest, and everyone knows her people were total pagans!*

WHO'S IN CHARGE OF BACKGROUND CHECKS?

So the first chick Matthew acknowledged in Jesus's family tree was a manipulative liar, the second was a prostitute, and the third had relatives straight out of an episode of *The Jerry Springer Show*. And Matthew won't even call the fourth woman by her given name. Instead, he describes her by saying, "Solomon's mother had been Uriah's wife" (Matthew 1:6, NCV).

You probably remember that Solomon's mama was the beautiful Bathsheba, with whom David had an affair before having her husband killed on the battlefield and marrying her.[6]

This list Matthew compiled is so *not* a group of good girls who had it all together.

Yet, through the deliberate inclusion of these women in Jesus's family tree, the God of the universe is essentially saying, "These are *my people!*" And God's mercy for these less-than-perfect women is especially significant in light of Matthew's original audience. The first readers of the gospel according to Matthew were Jewish men and women who'd been taught from birth that unless they followed, *to the letter,* each of the 613 commandments from the Torah (their version of the Holy Scriptures), they wouldn't be accepted—much less blessed—by Jehovah. And they earnestly believed perfection was a prerequisite to having a relationship with the coming Messiah.

But then along came Matt—a former IRS agent turned pastor—blowing their minds by teaching about the grace Immanuel extends to flawed people. I bet some of their faces lit up as they wondered, *Wow, if Jesus could associate with broken women like that, maybe He could accept me after all.* Matthew challenged their perception of the coming Messiah as a distant and demanding rule enforcer and presented a very different kind of Savior, one who compassionately associates with the most colorful of sinners.

From the very beginning this Savior brought into His most intimate circle women so disreputable that few of us would rush to claim them as friends. Women who had participated in or been a witness to appalling depravity were divinely embraced. Which is especially meaningful when you consider how desperate each one of the women in Matthew 1 must have been: Tamar needed a son so she'd have someone to care for her in her old age. Surely she felt cast aside, abandoned, worthless. As for Rahab, talk about a woman willing to take desperate measures, even betray her own people, to ensure her survival and that of her family. Ruth needed a kinsman-redeemer, someone to rescue her from desperate financial straits and cultural exclusion. Bathsheba, well, depending on your interpretation of the story, was either starving for affection or a deeply wronged woman forced to make the best of a horrific situation. These four probably would've settled for some small gesture of kindness…maybe a low-interest loan or a short reprieve from the mean-spirited gossip swirling about them. Instead, they were lovingly redeemed and literally woven into the family of God.

The *Wild* Ways of God

All four of the "wild girls" Matthew wove into the genealogy of Jesus experienced real-world redemption too: Tamar's father-in-law admitted he had mistreated her; as a result of risking her own life to assist the Israelites, Rahab was allowed to join them; Boaz married the widow Ruth, and their son Obed became the grandfather of King David; and David eventually took the blame for his adulterous liaison with Bathsheba and married her, making her one of his queens.[7]

I sometimes wonder if Isaiah was thinking about Tamar, Rahab, Ruth, or Bathsheba when he wrote these words:

"Don't be afraid, because you will not be ashamed.
    Don't be embarrassed, because you will not be
        disgraced.
You will forget the shame you felt earlier;
    you will not remember the shame you felt when
        you lost your husband.

The God who made you is like your husband.

His name is the LORD All-Powerful.

The Holy One of Israel is the one who saves you.

He is called the God of all the earth.

You were like a woman whose husband left her,

and you were very sad.

You were like a wife who married young·

and then her husband left her.

But the LORD called you to be his,"

says your God.

God says, "I left you for a short time,

but with great kindness I will bring you back again.

I became very angry

and hid from you for a time,

but I will show you mercy with kindness forever,"

says the LORD who saves you. *Isaiah 54:4–8, NCV*

The description is certainly apropos.

IT'S OKAY. SHE'S WITH ME.

At a crucial stage in my preadolescent development, my stepfather, John Angel, left the office of superintendent of the public school system in Seminole County, Florida, and became the principal of a state-of-the-art middle school about twenty miles from where we lived. He and Mom reasoned that since his new school had better resources than the one I was zoned to, it would be a good idea for me to transfer at the beginning of the sixth grade. Which sent absolute terror coursing through my preteen body.

I was already scared about graduating from elementary school to middle school. I'd heard rumors that you actually had to take off your clothes in front of everybody in P.E., that some kids smoked cigarettes in the bathroom, and that certain wild girls smuggled vodka in their Bonne Bell lip-gloss containers. Now to make matters worse, I was being dragged to a school where I didn't know anybody and where my step-father was the *principal*! It was as if the stars had aligned to make sure I became a miserable misfit.

And let me tell you, my first few days at Teague Middle School were indeed miserable. I felt like I'd crash-landed on some strange, inhospitable planet. The other students wore Levi cords and surf shirts, while I wore dress pants and button-up blouses. Most of the girls had blond "Farrah" hair, while mine was brown and wingless. They drank Cokes and ate snacks from the vending machines for lunch, while my brown paper sack contained healthy food like egg-salad sandwiches, squashed in Ziploc bags. It seemed everybody else had known each other since kindergarten as they jostled and joked between classes. I figured my best defense against outright rejection was to walk with my head down and hope no one would notice me.

But a few weeks later, somebody did: a grinning, tow-headed, athletic guy named Corky Clifton, the one all the guys wanted to be like and all the girls wanted to be with. For some reason he decided to step over the invisible line separating popular kids from pariahs and choose me—me!—as a friend. Because Corky took a risk to associate with the gawky new girl, I was warmly received into the often-hostile world of adolescence. Armed with Corky's seal of approval, I found that people scooted over so I'd have a place to sit at lunch. I got invited to pool parties. I had funny notes shoved into my locker.

Corky was willing to sacrifice his reputation as the coolest kid in the sixth grade by hanging out with me. Jesus was willing to sacrifice His *deity.* He knew the consequence of weaving His story with ours, and He still jumped at the chance. He forfeited His throne in heaven and boldly shrugged into a suit of skin.

Our Savior isn't some wimpy, pale guy wearing a caftan and Birkenstocks; He is our radically compassionate Savior who risked everything to restore mistake-prone people. He believes this motley crew called humanity is a treasure…that we're valuable enough to die for.

> *We need an* untamed *Savior because...*
> only a *wildly redemptive* Jesus can free us from the pain and bondage of past mistakes!

▪ ▪ Living and Loving with Abandon ▪ ▪

1. Which one of the four girls listed in Jesus's genealogy in Matthew 1 do you most identify with, and why?

2. Read Galatians 4:1–7. Describe the first time you realized you could call God "Father."

3. Read Isaiah 43:1–2. What mental picture best illustrates your response to God's redemptive declaration at the beginning of Isaiah 43?

4. Describe a situation in which someone sacrificed his or her reputation to redeem yours. How did it make you feel at the time? What about now?

5. If you were writing Jesus a literal thank-you note for choosing to hang out with you in spite of your mistakes and flaws, what would the first sentence be?

6. Read Philippians 2:1–11. Theologians have called verses 6–11 the "hymn of Christ." What do you think these New Testament lyrics suggest about how we should treat other people even if they don't have the right pedigree? Can you think of a pop-culture song with a similar anthem?

2

The God Who Leaves Men Gaping

Our Savior Is *Wildly* Unsettling

Left to ourselves we tend immediately
to reduce God to manageable terms.

—A. W. Tozer

■ ■ ■ ■ ■ ■

For the past several years, I've had a book deadline in July, so I spend most of June chained to my laptop, feverishly trying to create something readable. A few nights ago—in the midst of a hand-cramping, fanny-numbing writing marathon—I decided I needed a break. So I meandered outside and grabbed both ropes of my favorite swing. Then I ran backward to get as much *oomph* as possible and jumped on the seat as it began to catapult forward. Because this swing hangs from an old locust tree that sits on a little hill, if you get a really good backswing, you'll sail out over the drop-off quite a bit higher than an average rope swing.

Within moments I could feel my deadline-induced stress dissipating as I succumbed to the sweet smell of blooming magnolias and the lime green, Morse-code-like flashes of fireflies. After five or ten minutes of tranquillity, I remembered my friend Eva had called earlier, so I pulled the cell phone out of my pocket and dialed her number.

"Hey, Leeesa," she drawled, and I couldn't help grinning in response, because after almost three decades our friendship has grown as strong as her Southern accent. We chatted pleasantly about what we'd both been doing since we'd last seen each other—what she was teaching in Bible study, where I'd traveled, and the unique opportunities that present themselves when one spends a vacation with close relatives.

Our conversation was interrupted by a loud snort to my left as some *thing* came thundering down the hill toward me. In the dark it took a couple of seconds for me to recognize the charging shape as a cow. And its unexpected appearance was so disconcerting that, after it rushed past, all I could do was gape in open-mouthed wonder.

> What's the most recent surprise that left you so unsettled you couldn't even speak?

When I recovered my voice and explained to Eva that I'd just missed being trampled by a mad cow, she dissolved into laughter and sputtered, "Leeesa, a cow isn't gonna hurt you!" Of course I knew that. I actually spent a lot of time around cows when I was younger, because my dad raised cattle during his wannabe rancher years. I know that while bulls can be feisty, cows don't typically cause trouble. I just wasn't expecting one to come careening out of the night and interrupt my swing break.

Jesus has a way of jarring our expectations and shaking us out of complacency too. As a matter of fact, the second chapter of Luke reminds us that when He was just an adolescent—long before He silenced the seas or raised the dead or overturned tables—His otherworldliness was shocking. And while stampeding farm animals were probably a rarity in the temple courts, you can still bet the rabbis and scholars gaped in open-mouthed wonder when a twelve-year-old boy from a rural village called Nazareth began tutoring them in the finer points of Mosaic Law.

Even as a kid our Savior was *wildly unsettling*.

THE CASE OF THE MISSING MESSIAH

Before we explore Jesus's unnerving and precocious performance at the temple, let's back up and review the circumstances.

All mature Jewish males were obligated to go to Jerusalem three times a year to observe the three major religious festivals: Passover, Pentecost, and the Feast of Tabernacles.[1] However, after Israel was divided as a nation and God's people were dispersed geographically, it became financially difficult for most Jews to obey this command literally. Therefore thousands of families (the wife and kids in observant families usually made the pilgrimage as well) began going to the Holy City just once a year to celebrate the big kahuna of festivals, *Passover*. This was the case with Jesus's family:

> Every year Jesus' parents went to Jerusalem for the Passover
> Feast. When he was twelve years old, they went to the feast as
> they always did. After the feast days were over, they started
> home. The boy Jesus stayed behind in Jerusalem, but his par-
> ents did not know it. Thinking that Jesus was with them in
> the group, they traveled for a whole day. Then they began to
> look for him among their family and friends. When they did
> not find him, they went back to Jerusalem to look for him
> there. *Luke 2:41–45, NCV*

After camping in Jerusalem for a week or so and celebrating both Passover and the Feast of Unleavened Bread with friends and family, Joseph and Mary packed up the tent and began the long walk home to Galilee. Because caravans to and from the temple were normally made up of people from the same city or village,[2] Joseph and Mary assumed

Jesus was somewhere among the crowd of dusty travelers as they hiked out of Jerusalem. They probably thought He was tossing a football around with some of His cousins. They didn't realize He was missing for an entire day.

I'm sure Mary's face was tense with worry on the trek back to Jerusalem to find her misplaced son. As soon as she and Joseph got to the edge of the Holy City, she pulled Jesus's middle school picture—the one that showed His cowlick and braces—out of her wallet and began asking everyone if they'd seen Him. She and Joseph anxiously knocked on doors, retraced their steps, and put fliers on windshields. By late afternoon they'd exhausted every lead, and her mother's heart was heavy. She sat down wearily on a rock wall and began to weep.

Joseph watched his wife's shoulders shake with grief for several agonizing minutes. Suddenly he leaped to his feet and cried, "Hey, Mar, I'll bet He's at the temple!" They hurried across town, raced up the uneven temple steps two at a time, and burst into a classroom to finally find their son sitting cross-legged on the floor, teaching a group of dumbfounded men five and six times His age!

> After three days they found him in the temple, sitting among
> the teachers, listening to them and asking them questions.
> And all who heard him were amazed at his understanding and
> his answers. *Luke 2:46–47*

The expressions on Mary's and Joseph's faces transformed from worry to relief when they found Jesus, but I'll bet the rabbis and scholars listening to His lecture still appeared shocked, because the word *amazed* falls short in translating the utter astonishment implied by the

Greek word used in the original manuscripts of Luke's gospel, which is *existēmi*. And it literally means "to remove oneself" or to figuratively "go out of one's mind."[3]

Those religious intellectuals weren't just a tad surprised by Jesus's knowledge and insight; they nearly had mental meltdowns, because it was too much for them to grasp that this boy's brain housed the mind of God! This brow-raising event was one of the first tangible clues that the Alpha and Omega had graciously distilled His omniscience into His Son.

■ ■ ■ ■ ■ ■ The *Wild* Ways of God ■ ■ ■ ■ ■ ■

When discussing the concept of Jesus being as smart as His heavenly Dad, you can use the fancy phrase *ontological equality* to impress your friends. It basically means that the three members of the Trinity—Father, Son, and Holy Spirit—are equal in their being.[4]

Unsettling Doesn't Mean Disrespectful or Arrogant

My friend Kim's youngest child, Benji, has a very strong personality and isn't shy about verbalizing his opinion. After a recent exchange with her sometimes-impertinent boy, she and I started chatting about how much parenting has changed since we were kids. If we'd said things like, "That's *so* lame" in reference to something our mothers had said or done, we would have been swatted repeatedly with a switch—which we'd personally selected from a tree in the backyard so as to add insult to injury—until welts formed on the backs of our legs. Then we'd have been grounded for a month. Our mamas did not tolerate smart-alecky offspring!

When you read about Mary and Joseph crashing Jesus's teaching party in the temple, His response might initially seem switch-worthy:

> When Jesus' parents saw him, they were astonished. His
> mother said to him, "Son, why did you do this to us? Your
> father and I were very worried about you and have been
> looking for you."
> Jesus said to them, "Why were you looking for me?
> Didn't you know that I must be in my Father's house?"
> *Luke 2:48–49, NCV*

I can totally imagine Joseph getting red in the face and bellowing in one of those deep, scary-daddy voices, "*What* did you just say to your mother?" But Joseph didn't blow his top, and Jesus certainly wasn't being a brat; He was simply reminding His mother and stepfather of the obvious. One of my favorite modern-day Bible scholars, Dr. Charles Swindoll, puts it this way:

> Upon first glance, Jesus' answer might appear a tad sassy, but
> we can't hear the inflection of His voice in print. He was gen-
> uinely confused by their searching for three days before look-
> ing in the temple. If they had remembered His beginnings or
> recalled the words of Simeon, the temple should have been
> their first place to look upon returning to Jerusalem. Where
> else would the Son of God be but in the house of God?[5]

As I reflect further on this scene between Jesus and His earthly parents, it occurs to me that if I were the smartest person in the world, I'd want at least a few people to be impressed. Not that I would necessarily post my academic stats on Facebook, but I wouldn't protest if someone else did. I'm quite sure I'd attempt to insert the periodic table and facts about string theory into everyday conversation. I would also accost non-English-speaking tourists just to prove to passersby that I was multilingual. And I would probably roll my eyes when others made an observation I considered to be incorrect or obvious. In short, I would be a brilliant bore!

However, our Savior is not like me and didn't feel the need to flaunt His unprecedented brainpower:

And they did not understand the saying that he spoke to them. And he went down with them and came to Nazareth and was submissive to them. *Luke 2:50–51*

In other words, in spite of the fact that Jesus was infinitely smarter than His parents—*who did not understand the saying that he spoke to them*—He submitted to them. He didn't roll His eyes and say, "Can't you see I'm doing superimportant stuff here?" Nor did He treat them with condescension by suggesting, "Why don't y'all go get a bite to eat at the Falafel House, and I'll text you when I'm about to wrap up things here." According to Luke's account of this event (which Mary probably described to him[6]), Jesus got up, followed His confused parents back home to Nazareth, and continued acquiescing to their altogether ordinary authority.

I can't wrap my dinky, finite mind around the concept of omniscience—of *knowing everything*—much less understand what it's like to be the sharpest tool in the universe's shed yet still choose to defer to others out of love. Although Jesus probably understood His calling and true identity before He started shaving, He didn't groan when Mary mispronounced a big word or try to tutor Joseph in the physics of carpentry and construction. Instead, "He remained humble and silent until the proper time."[7] Which is also disconcerting. I mean, how many teenagers do you know who would not only yield willingly to their parents but also resist the urge to demonstrate their verbal sparring skills?

■ ■ ■ ■ ■ ■ ■ The *Wild* Ways of God ■ ■ ■ ■ ■ ■ ■

Although the New Testament sayings of Jesus are typically recorded in Greek, that was not His original language. His native tongue was Aramaic—more specifically, a Galilean version of western Aramaic. Luke 4:16-20 reveals that Jesus also read and spoke Hebrew.[8] Of course, since He's omniscient—*all knowing*—Jesus can converse in and understand every language and dialect. He is mega-multilingual!

RECURRENT WONDER

Several months ago I was invited to be on the *Life Today* television show with James and Betty Robison. During the interview they asked me to relate a story that happened many years ago at the end of a large Christian women's conference in the Midwest. Kathy Troccoli was leading worship at this particular event, and she concluded by inviting women in need of prayer to come forward to the platform while she sang a song based on Psalm 23.

Now, I truly believe that inviting individuals to pray is almost always a good thing, but you know how people sometimes get whipped into an emotive frenzy in spiritual settings? Well, this was one of those times. Over a thousand women surged forward and began to cry and carry on and loudly express their distress. Personally, I'm a firm believer in weeping before the Lord—even whining if you need to. And I appreciate God's assurance that He counts our troubles and stores our tears.[9] Scripture makes it clear that no sincere grief on our part is ever ignored by our heavenly Father.

However, much of the sorrow expressed at this conference seemed to be more self-induced than Holy Spirit–generated, and I found myself thinking, *Wow, we need to do something to shift the focus back to God's goodness and away from our misery!* Kathy was thinking the same thing, because when she wrapped up the song, she marched over to where I was hovering at the edge of the stage, shoved the microphone toward me, and said authoritatively, "Pray, Lisa!"

A little flustered by all the drama, I wasn't sure exactly where to begin. But I've found that even much smaller groups of women typically include a few who are struggling in their marriage, some who are worried about prodigal children, others who are suffering with cancer, and sadly at least a handful who've recently lost someone they loved. So I simply started praying some of God's promises: that He's near to the brokenhearted and saves those who are crushed in spirit, that His name is a strong tower, and the righteous can run to it and find refuge.[10] Just as I was getting on a roll, I sensed God tap me on the shoulder and tell me to pray something else. Now I didn't hear God's audible voice as Abraham or Moses did, but the voice in my head was unmistakably His. John 10:1–5 assures Christians we can recognize our Redeemer's voice. And I couldn't ignore it.

I have to admit, however, that I *wanted* to ignore it, because I was certain the words He was impressing me to pray would be about as welcome as a vegan at a National Cattlemen's conference. I couldn't help thinking, *They killed prophets in the Old Testament, Lord. May I please just say "Amen" and be done with it?*

Yet God's Spirit continued poking me so insistently that I knew it'd be overt disobedience to refuse His request. So I prayed for women who were struggling with their sexuality and living in lesbian relationships. Yeah, I know. It's not a prayer you hear very often in a setting where most women are wearing matching purses and shoes. I don't remember any details about what happened immediately after my prayer that day. At least no one pelted me with rocks, and within a few hours I was safely on a plane headed back to Nashville.

A few weeks later I received a letter from a young woman named Karen who'd been at the event. She explained that she'd been attending that conference for years, not because she enjoyed it, but to appease her mother. Karen had been raised in a Christian home but rebelled in college through excessive drinking, promiscuity, and homosexual relationships. Since she lived on the other side of the state from her conservative mama, she'd been able to keep her prodigal ways a secret.

Karen wrote, "I don't know if you remember, but the prayer time at the end of the conference was really emotional."

Yeah, I remember!

As all those women gathered around the platform that day, Karen had stayed put in her top-row seat at the back of the convention center with her arms crossed and thinking, *Ugh, I hate this! These women are a bunch of dramatic hypocrites, and nothing that's been said all day applies to me.* In that moment, she wrote in her letter, she sort of dared God to show up by praying silently, *God, if you're real, I dare you to make that lady*—she had no idea who I was—*say the word "lesbian," because I've been here seven years in a row and haven't heard anybody talk about what I'm walking through.*

Seconds later, when I said that word in my prayer, she was so shocked that she bolted out of her seat and escaped to the bathroom, where she stayed until the conference was completely over. Then she walked out to her car by herself, feeling overwhelmed, isolated, and unsure of how to handle what seemed to be an answer from a God she'd nearly stopped believing in.

A week later Karen was driving down the highway in anguish because she'd lost her job and her latest girlfriend in quick succession. Despairing of her very life, she cried out to God and basically asked Him the same thing she had the previous weekend. "God, if you're real, please help me find you." After her candid request, she absent-mindedly turned on her radio and was surprised to hear Kathy Troccoli singing the same song she'd sung at the end of the conference. Karen explained that she never listened to inspirational music and wasn't sure how her stereo got tuned in to that station! Then, even more astonishing, instead of a deejay's voice or a commercial coming on when the song was over, the station aired my prayer, and she heard *that word* a second time. She described the experience as being so unsettling—and so *unmistakably God*—that she felt compelled to pull her car over to the shoulder of the road and ask Jesus to forgive her and take control of her life.

As I recently shared Karen's story with James and Betty, I felt my heart gaping in wonder all over again at our Savior, at what lengths He goes to draw heartbroken people to Himself. It reawakened my amazement.

Luke tells us that Mary's experience of finding her young son tutoring religious leaders in the temple provided fresh astonishment for her too:

And his mother treasured up all these things in her heart.
Luke 2:51

You may remember this as Mary's second treasure hunt; she'd had the very same experience after giving birth to Jesus:

When the angels went away from them into heaven, the shepherds said to one another, "Let us go over to Bethlehem and see this thing that has happened, which the Lord has made known to us." And they went with haste and found Mary and Joseph, and the baby lying in a manger. And when they saw it, they made known the saying that had been told them concerning this child. And all who heard it wondered at what the shepherds told them. *But Mary treasured up all these things, pondering them in her heart. Luke 2:15–19, emphasis added*

Which means that, as a teenage mother, Mary truly contemplated the miracle that her newborn son was Immanuel...*God with us.* In fact, I'll bet she mused constantly in those first few weeks after Jesus's manger debut. She probably walked around in a state of open-mouthed bewilderment, thinking, *Why in the world did Jehovah choose Joseph and me to be His mom and dad? We don't have any parenting skills. Oh man, I've only baby-sat once or twice... What if I accidentally drop the Lion of Judah on His little pink head?* Surely her eyes filled with awed tears the first time Christ incarnate grabbed her pinkie in His chubby fist or when His eyes found hers while He nursed.

But life goes on, and soon Mary was spending more time doing laundry, fixing meals, and helping Joseph design a Web page for his business than marveling about her son, the Messiah. Before she knew it, Mary had four more energetic sons along with several daughters clamoring for her attention and affection.[11] She barely had time to run a comb through her hair each morning, much less think about how their oldest was going to redeem the world. Twelve years later the shepherds' prophecy in Bethlehem had all but faded from her mortal mind...until she saw the wide-eyed expressions of the temple scholars who were hanging on to her little man's every word. And that's when Jesus's own mama was amazed all over again.

Too Wonderful for Comprehension

If you dig deep enough, you'll find that the Gospels reveal much about Christ's life and ministry that is mind-boggling. His heritage is supernatural, yet He allowed it to be sullied with humanity. His mind contained the wisdom of the ages, yet sometimes He chose to veil His omniscience with genuine curiosity. He got physically tired and hungry, yet contained within His Spirit the power of the resurrection. He was born in Bethlehem two thousand years ago, yet John says Jesus was present with God before time began: He was "in the beginning with God" (John 1:2).

■ ■ ■ ■ ■ ■ ■ The *Wild* Ways of God ■ ■ ■ ■ ■ ■ ■

Jesus was incarnate: both God and man. Therefore He had human intellect *and* divine omniscience. But just as His body had human limitations—Jesus got tired, hungry, thirsty, and He bled when cut—the Bible reveals there were situations in which He chose to limit His omniscience.[12]

It does us tremendous good to ponder these vast mysteries about Jesus, because in so doing we gain perspective and appreciation. It's like what happens when you sprawl out in the grass on a clear night and look up at the stars. Staring at the stars—more important, meditating on the One who named each fiery orb and hung it in the sky—is a great reminder that God is grander than we can logically comprehend.

And while it's unsettling to consider our finite lives in light of His infinite power and glory, it's a *good* kind of unsettling. It prompts us to ponder how being loved by our Trinitarian Redeemer and being included in His eternal plans is bigger and better than what we can see, think, or even feel.

Plus, gazing at His unfathomable majesty recalibrates our hearts to their original, proper settings. The lever set on "drudgery" moves to "joy," the knob set for "depression" clicks toward "hope," the switch set on "unworthy" flips to "adored," and the dial set on "bondage" spins toward "freedom"!

We need an untamed *Savior because...*
only a *wildly unsettling* Jesus can free us to be amazed by His grace!

▪ ▪ Living and Loving with Abandon ▪ ▪

1. Besides stargazing, what other activities help you ponder the unfathomable majesty of Christ?

2. Read Genesis 1:26–27 and John 1:1–18. How would you explain to a child these complex passages—illustrating that God is a Trinitarian "Us" and He existed as God the Father, Son, and Holy Spirit from the beginning?

3. Read Isaiah 55:8–9. What metaphor would you use in place of "as the heavens are higher than the earth" to paraphrase this verse?

4. Read Psalm 139:1–4; Job 21:22; Romans 11:33–34; and Hebrews 4:13. What main point do these verses make about God's "mind"?

5. Read Mark 6:45–52. The disciples were so unsettled by Jesus's majesty in this situation that they thought He was a ghost! When have you been so astounded by Him that it scared you a little?

6. Read Romans 11:33–36. What adjective would you use to describe the theme of Paul's doxology? How has God's unsettling inscrutability led to worship in your life?

3

The Very Best Friend
of All

Our Savior Is *Wildly* Devoted

God loves us: not because we are loveable but
because He is love, not because He needs to
receive but because He delights to give.

—C. S. LEWIS

I used to love climbing on the junglegym in our backyard. It was a twelve-foot high, open-framed, steel-tube contraption shaped like a pyramid. I haven't seen one like it in a long time; they probably quit manufacturing them because of litigation involving the inevitable falls that occur when children are allowed to clamber around on rickety scaffolding. I had the wind knocked out of me quite a few times myself! But by far the worst injury I sustained while scaling that outdated playground equipment was a broken heart.

Late one afternoon my best friend at the time—a five-year-old comrade who lived directly behind us—and I were pretending the junglegym was our castle. We were both princesses, cooing entreaties down to imaginary princes, when we were interrupted by her mother calling her to the fence that separated our houses. Sally (not her real name) scrambled down from our turret and sheepishly walked over to her mom.

Sally's mom was a big, bossy woman who scared me a little. She had three particularly intimidating habits: she yelled a lot, she stomped when she walked, and she almost always wore too-tight, garishly bright Bermuda shorts. So I just continued to play quietly and didn't glance over while she reprimanded Sally. But since her whisper was as loud as her apparel, I could hear every word she said. And what came through her clenched teeth is still vivid all these years later. "Sally, you come home this minute! Mr. and Mrs. Harper are getting divorced, so you can't play with Lisa anymore. That little girl is trash!"

> Have you ever been branded as not good
> enough to be friends with someone?

Sally looked back over her shoulder at me as she scurried toward her mother, and I can't remember if her expression was one of apology or pity. I do remember feeling shame. I was deeply embarrassed to be regarded as inferior and different from the other kids in our one-divorce neighborhood. Her snub left me longing for a *true* friend, someone who would stick by me no matter what.

Unlike humans, who tend to be a bit fickle in their affections, Jesus is totally devoted to us *no matter what.* He is resolute in His relational commitments, hanging on to those He loves with the tenacity of a bulldog guarding a juicy bone. Incredibly, the only Man who really was superior to everyone else never played the "I'm too good for you" card. He didn't make fun of teammates who struck out in T-ball. He didn't mock schoolmates with noticeable lisps. And He sure didn't snub pals whose parents were splitting up.

As a friend, Jesus is *wildly devoted.*

BUDDIES BEFORE BIRTH

John the Baptist was Jesus's second cousin and oldest friend. They actually met before they were born, and John was so excited by the encounter that he did some prenatal gymnastics:

44

In those days Mary arose and went with haste into the hill country, to a town in Judah, and she entered the house of Zechariah and greeted Elizabeth. And when Elizabeth heard the greeting of Mary, the baby leaped in her womb. And Elizabeth was filled with the Holy Spirit, and she exclaimed with a loud cry, "Blessed are you among women, and blessed is the fruit of your womb! And why is this granted to me that the mother of my Lord should come to me? For behold, when the sound of your greeting came to my ears, the baby in my womb leaped for joy." *Luke 1:39–44*

Jesus and John the Baptist surely climbed junglegyms together when they were young and their moms chatted over coffee, but they didn't see much of each other during their teens and twenties because John moved out to the Judean desert, probably after being orphaned by the deaths of his elderly parents:

And the child grew and became strong in spirit, and he was in the wilderness until the day of his public appearance to Israel. *Luke 1:80*

So while Jesus was growing up in a noisy household with two loving parents and a gaggle of brothers and sisters, John came of age in the austere silence of the wilderness. While Jesus conversed with rabbis and celebrated religious festivals, John fasted and prayed in solitude. And the older they grew, the odder John seemed to get. Not only did he abstain from socializing and alcohol (dutifully following the instructions an angel gave his dad before he was born[1]), but he also began wearing putrid animal skins, eating bugs and honey, and preaching fire-and-brimstone sermons that made his audience squirm.[2]

■ ■ ■ ■ ■ ■ The *Wild* Ways of God ■ ■ ■ ■ ■ ■

Many biblical historians believe John the Baptist spent time with the Essenes of Qumran, a monastic sect who'd left Jerusalem in a huff to protest the hypocrisy and politics they felt were infecting Judaism. They were an ascetic group whose stoic dedication to preserving the Torah resulted in the Dead Sea Scrolls, the earliest written copies we have of the Old Testament.

In his classic book *The Prisoner in the Third Cell,* pastor and master storyteller Gene Edwards describes Johnny B like this:

The nomadic caravans were the first to come face-to-face with the desert prophet. Their eyes registered unbelief as they gazed upon the sight of such an emaciated creature. Their first thought was simple enough. "He is some madman who wandered into the desert." Or, more charitably, "The heat has driven one of the Essenes quite mad."

Obviously this nameless man was a Jew; but he wore the garment of an unclean animal, the loathsome camel. And it was soon rumored that for food he ate locusts—a food used by only the poorest, most impoverished people.

His outward appearance declared him a lunatic; his words

declared him a prophet. His hair, unkept, reached almost to his knees. His face was that of an old man, but his voice thundered with the vigor of youth. His eyes flashed the burning fire of the desert.[3]

Rationally speaking, it would've made sense for Jesus to avoid John the Baptist. Hanging out with a smelly fanatic could definitely have harmed His Messianic reputation. But of course our perfectly reliable Redeemer did just the opposite.

A SINNER DOES THE DUNKING

Proverbs speaks of "a friend who sticks closer than a brother" (Proverbs 18:24, NIV), and that's who Jesus was to John the Baptist. Although at this point in his ministry many people considered John more eccentric than prophetic, our Savior—the Son of the Living God—walked down to the bank of the Jordan River, where John was baptizing folks, and said, in essence, "Hey, Cuz, how about dunking me under, too?"

> Jesus then appeared, arriving at the Jordan River from Galilee. He wanted John to baptize him. *Matthew 3:13, MSG*

Several years ago I got to speak at an event with Jill Briscoe, who is one of my all-time favorite Bible teachers. In my estimation she's the female equivalent of Billy Graham or Charles Spurgeon. Plus, she has an elegant British accent, which makes her sound even smarter! I didn't talk much when we ate dinner together before the program started, mainly because I didn't trust myself not to gush or say something stupid. After dinner a hostess escorted me to the front of the noisy auditorium, where hundreds of women were excitedly gathered, and loud music was pulsating through the sound system. I sat down and got situated, pulling my Bible out of my purse and placing it on the seat beside me.

Minutes later Jill was ushered up to the front. She smiled, raised her eyebrows, and gestured at the seat next to me as a way of asking, "May I sit there?" since we couldn't hear each other speak over the din. I smiled back and nodded, quickly picking my Bible off the chair while thinking, *This is so cool. I can't believe I'm getting to sit next to Jill Briscoe!* But then she paused and shifted over, one seat removed from me. I was so disappointed that she'd put distance between us, and for a moment I wondered if she wasn't as nice in person as she seemed behind the podium.

That uncharitable thought vanished when I looked down to see a bright purple feminine-hygiene product resting on the chair between us. (Fortunately it was still wrapped in its original packaging.) It had obviously stuck to my Bible when it was in my purse and then adhered itself to the seat when I snatched the Bible back up. Jill had graciously moved over so as not to call attention to my gaffe. I felt like a mangy mutt beside a Westminster Kennel Club champion!

I wonder if that's kind of how John the Baptist felt when Jesus slipped off His sandals and started wading into the water. John, who's referred to as God's "messenger" in the last book of the Old Testament,[4] sure appeared to be feeling unworthy and flustered when he held up his hands and said, "Wait a minute, Jesus. This isn't how it's supposed to go down. You're the Lamb of God; You're supposed to be baptizing me!"

> But John tried to talk him out of it. "I am the one who needs to be baptized by you," he said, "so why are you coming to me?" *Matthew 3:14, NLT*

And John the Baptist wasn't the only one discombobulated by Christ's decision to splash into the Jordan. To this day, people question why the Messiah chose to get wet since baptism is a sign of repentance, and Jesus was not a sinner.[5] The basic answer to the complicated question of why He got baptized is that Jesus submitted to the ritual cleansing in order to connect the dots between John (His "advance man") and Himself, as well as to identify with human sinners like us, who desperately need a hero's footsteps to follow in.

Furthermore, when Jesus humbly asked John to lower Him into a muddy stream for His official inauguration, He was endorsing that hairy hermit's ministry. Now that's an awesome ally!

■ ■ ■ ■ ■ ■ The *Wild* Ways of God ■ ■ ■ ■ ■ ■

Although the Jordan River is often mentioned in the Bible—and sung about in old hymns—it's not a very impressive stream by statistical standards. It flows approximately 135 miles south from the Sea of Galilee, which is actually a lake, to the Dead Sea. It rarely exceeds ten feet in depth and only averages thirty yards in width.[6] Both times I've visited Israel, it was noticeably muddy. Which is why Naaman was offended when Elisha told him to rinse in the Jordan seven times in order to be cured from leprosy instead of going for a dip in one of the beautiful brooks of his native land.[7] Just another example of God's delight in using unlikely means to carry out His divine purposes.

A FAIL-SAFE FRIEND

Corinne Barfield is one of my dearest allies. We met twenty years ago when I was a brand-new youth leader trying to get a Bible study started at her high school, and we've been buddies ever since. However, judging from a recent conversation, I'm sure time will prove her to be a better friend to me than I am to her. Somehow we got to talking about loyalty, and Corinne sincerely exclaimed—as only a critical-care nurse such as she could (or would), "Lisa, you can always count on me. Even if you get really sick and your hair falls out and you're bedridden and you have to wear diapers, I'll stay right by your side through it all. I'm here for the long haul."

I wanted to reply, "Me too," but our relationship has been totally honest from the beginning, and I couldn't lie. You see, I have a sensitive gag reflex. Sometimes I accidentally gag myself simply brushing my teeth. I would totally be there for Corinne when it came to tying on turbans, keeping a bedside vigil, mowing her lawn, and making chicken soup. But the mere thought of someone else's bodily fluids makes my eyes water. So I assured Corinne I'd do my absolute best to stick by her side no matter what but confessed there's a distinct possibility I'll get a bit wobbly if the going gets really rough!

The going got really rough for John the Baptist not long after he baptized Jesus. During one of his straightforward sermons, he publicly denounced Herod Antipas's love affair and subsequent marriage to Herodias as the ungodly, incestuous mess that it was. She was still married to Herod Antipas's half-brother when they got the hots for each other. When the ruler of Galilee and Perea (also called Herod the tetrarch) got wind of John's indictment, he had him roughed up, tied up, and tossed in jail.[8] While John was rotting away in that dank cell, he got a little wobbly:

> After Jesus finished telling these things to his twelve followers, he left there and went to the towns in Galilee to teach and preach.
>
> John the Baptist was in prison, but he heard about what the Christ was doing. So John sent some of his followers to Jesus. They asked him, "Are you the One who is to come, or should we wait for someone else?" *Matthew 11:1–3, NCV*

In other words, John was asking Jesus, "Are You really the Messiah? I mean, good night, here I've been slaving away in the desert without wine, women, or ESPN, and You're going to parties, hanging out with drunks and prostitutes, and telling people to love those who persecute them. I thought You were supposed to come out swinging and spewing fire!"

I guess it's understandable that John's dedication wavered. I mean, he was wasting away in prison. Plus, Jehovah had impressed him to prophesy the following words about a harsher hero than he'd witnessed thus far in Jesus:

> I baptize you with water for repentance, but he who is coming after me is mightier than I, whose sandals I am not worthy to carry. He will baptize you with the Holy Spirit and fire. His winnowing fork is in his hand, and he will clear his threshing floor and gather his wheat into the barn, but the chaff he will burn with unquenchable fire. *Matthew 3:11–12*

■ ■ ■ ■ ■ ■ The *Wild* Ways of God ■ ■ ■ ■ ■ ■

John the Baptist fulfilled Isaiah's and Malachi's prophecies about the messenger who would come to prepare the way for the Lord (Isaiah 40:3; Malachi 3:1). In addition, both of John's parents were from priestly lineage, further legitimizing him as a holy man.[9]

But still. Don't you think this guy should've at least been reprimanded for doubting the divinity of the Lord? Most friendships would be irreparably severed by such questions. Yet Jesus didn't condemn His cousin; instead, He grabbed a megaphone, began a "Johnny B" cheer, and incited the crowd into doing the wave:

Jesus replied, "Go back and report to John what you hear and see: The blind receive sight, the lame walk, those who have leprosy are cured, the deaf hear, the dead are raised, and the good news is preached to the poor. Blessed is the man who does not fall away on account of me."

As John's disciples were leaving, Jesus began to speak to the crowd about John: "What did you go out into the desert to see? A reed swayed by the wind? If not, what did you go out to see? A man dressed in fine clothes? No, those who wear fine clothes are in kings' palaces. Then what did you go out to see? A prophet? Yes, I tell you, and more than a prophet. This is the one about whom it is written:

" 'I will send my messenger ahead of you,

who will prepare your way before you.'

"I tell you the truth: Among those born of women there has not risen anyone greater than John the Baptist." *Matthew 11:4–11, NIV*

Our Savior chose friends who didn't make sense on paper. I would've assumed that God incarnate would pair Himself with more impressive associates. Definitely not guys with locust legs stuck between their teeth. But Jesus is the friend who lovingly sticks by every repentant sinner's side through thick and thin. Even when we blow it or get distracted by other interests, He doesn't stop loving us. In fact, Jesus's unwavering commitment to us is what ultimately compelled Him to lay down His life in exchange for ours.

His devotion to broken people like us is remarkable. Some would even call it wild.

We need an untamed *Savior because...* only a *wildly devoted* Jesus can free us from worrying if He'll ditch us for a cooler cast of friends or walk away when we don't hold up our end of the relationship.

▪ ▪ Living and Loving with Abandon ▪ ▪

1. Describe the most intensely devout Christian you know. Do you tend to be more attracted to or repulsed by his or her commitment?

2. For you, what would be the hardest part of practicing spiritual asceticism as John the Baptist did: giving up creature comforts or seeing the raised eyebrows of people who think you're a nut?

3. Read Matthew 3:7–12. How would you summarize the main theme of John the Baptist's sermon? In what ways do you think his message would differ if he were still preaching today?

4. Read Isaiah 42:3. How has Jesus protected your "flickering flame" or braced the "bruised reed" part of you?

5. Describe a recent situation in which someone has been a loyal friend to you when you've been less than deserving.

6. Read Isaiah 61:1–2. Why do you think Jesus quoted from this particular Old Testament prophecy to encourage John?

4

Rough, Tough, and Ready to Rumble

Our Savior Is *Wildly* Tough

Jesus perseveres on the straight and narrow in spite of the temptation, but one senses that his endurance is hard-won.

—SUSAN GARRETT

■ ■ ■ ■ ■ ■

After my parents divorced, I spent most weekends when I was in elementary and middle school at my dad's farm in central Florida. We had a menagerie of animals, and we had Honda dirt bikes to roam the nearby fields and orange groves, so it was a paradise with endless opportunities for mischief for a thrill-seeking tomboy like me!

One of my favorite naughty adventures was a game I called "Psych the Cows." First, I'd talk my less-adventurous stepbrother, Ricky, into climbing a tree in a clump of woods in the middle of the cow pasture. Then I'd prance out toward our herd of Holsteins and shake a coffee can full of sweet feed. Since that was the "dinner bell" our dad used to get them to come to the barn to eat, they'd look up from their grazing and begin to lumber toward me.

As they drew closer, they would begin speeding up to stampede velocity. I'd stand my ground until the cows started closing in, then I'd sprint toward the low-hanging branch where Ricky sat with a look of horror. Squealing with glee and the thrill of danger, I'd leap up, grab his limb, and swing to safety just as the cows thundered beneath us!

The only real bummer about this game—other than Ricky's being scarred for life—was that the cows fell for the feed-can scam only once or twice each weekend. After that, they calmly chewed their cud and wouldn't even glance my way when I tried to lure them toward the woods. (A few of them obviously complained about my cruel trickery to their calves, who told their calves, who told their calves, until whole generations of cows across America knew about it, and that's probably the explanation for the revenge run-by I mentioned in a previous chapter.)

One Saturday after several failed attempts to provoke the cows into pursuit, I exclaimed to a wary Ricky, "Hey, let's go psych the bull!" He strongly objected and reminded me that Dad had explicitly warned us not to go anywhere near that Texas Longhorn bull. I assured Ricky we wouldn't get close to the bull; we'd practice our silent Indian walk and sneak through the woods to the opposite side of the field, where he always grazed alone (the bull had proved too dangerous to breed, so Dad had sequestered him to a pasture by himself), thereby giving us a huge head start. Ricky was reluctant, but after some enthusiastic begging, I finally got him to fall in behind me—way behind me.

What I didn't know was that the bull had changed chewing spots.

When I stepped from the woods into the clearing, I came face to face with the beast. Nostrils flaring, he pawed the ground with his front hoofs, then lowered his horns and charged. I screamed, spun around, and sprinted for the fence. Somehow I managed to stay a few feet in front of the bull (Ricky had been lagging so far behind that he easily escaped calamity), but as the fence loomed closer, I realized I wouldn't have time to crawl through the barbed wire. So I aimed for the closest post and tried to vault over. But when my feet hit the top strand, the U-shaped nail holding the wire in place popped loose, and one of the barbs pierced my backside, effectively skewering me in place.

I tensed with dread, expecting to become the next notch on that Longhorn's belt. But then Dad raced up. I was shocked to see him, because the last I knew, he'd been busy in the barn, several hundred yards away. I still don't know how he got there so fast, but I instinctively knew that his arrival meant everything was going to be okay. And it was. Dad steadied me with one hand and began punching the bull in the nose with the other, eventually convincing the beast to turn away in defeat. Then he hooked my arms around his neck, hoisted me off the fence, and carried me to the house to make sure I wasn't seriously injured.

Although I knew I'd soon feel the sting of alcohol where I'd been jabbed, and I'd have to endure a very long lecture, I couldn't help grinning, because *my* dad went toe-to-toe with a bull and won!

> What's the bravest thing your father—or a
> father figure—has ever done on your behalf?

I think I'm even more impressed with Dad's heroics now that I'm an adult. Since I'm an inch taller than he is, I realize he didn't have the raw physical ability to simply overpower that hunk of beef. The bull outweighed him by well over a thousand pounds. But what Dad lacked in brute strength, he made up for in fierce determination and grit. Pound for pound, my father is as tough as they come.

Our Savior probably wasn't a superbig, strapping man either. In fact, the Old Testament prophet Isaiah describes Jesus as having "no form or majesty that we should look at him, and no beauty that we should desire him" (Isaiah 53:2).

Yet immeasurably more so than even my dad, our Redeemer is *wildly tough.*

Popeye Would've Been Jealous

Not much is written about Jesus from the time of His teaching premiere at the temple, when He was twelve, until His cousin John the Baptist baptized Him, when He was around thirty.[1] All we know for sure is that He obeyed His parents and grew in wisdom and physical maturity.[2] We can also safely assume Jesus apprenticed with His stepfather, Joseph, as a *tektōn*, which most English Bibles translate as "carpenter."[3]

However, the literal definition of that Greek word *tektōn* is actually broader and can be translated as "builder."[4] Since Israel is arid and doesn't have very many large hardwood trees (remember Solomon had to have cedar timbers floated in from Lebanon when the temple was being constructed[5]), it's likely that Joseph and Jesus actually worked as stonemasons in the bustling metropolis of Sepphoris, which was just three miles north of Nazareth.[6]

But whether Jesus carried a lunch pail and hiked alongside Joseph to Sepphoris with a backpack full of chiseling tools or whether His forearms were covered in sawdust when He emerged from their woodworking shop in the backyard to clean up for dinner, He *grew up*. And by the time Jesus was a man, He was one tough cookie, which is abundantly clear from the very beginning of His scuffle with Satan in the wilderness:

> Next Jesus was taken into the wild by the Spirit for the Test.
> The Devil was ready to give it. Jesus prepared for the Test by
> fasting forty days and forty nights. *Matthew 4:1–2*, MSG

The Holy Spirit whispered to Jesus that He and Lucifer were going to square off in a title bout. So it would've made sense for Jesus to ramp up His caloric intake, right? Maybe ask Mary to start adding a couple of extra pancakes to His stack every morning and chug a protein smoothie every night. Surely He needed to add some bulk to His mediocre (according to Isaiah) body in order to last ten rounds with the Prince of Darkness. Instead, Jesus fasted for more than a month. He went without food to focus intently on spiritual preparation.

I really can't imagine not eating for that long; I have a hard time skipping a meal. And don't forget, our Redeemer was incarnate. Although divine, He chose to accept the restrictions of a flesh-and-blood body. That means Jesus didn't morph into an intangible mist before facing the enemy. He experienced the same headaches and dizziness and stomach cramps we would if we didn't have any nourishment for forty straight days. Just thinking about it makes me want to go rummage around in the refrigerator.

So in spite of His ordinary physique, Jesus had extraordinary fortitude; He was *physically tough*.

■ ■ ■ ■ ■ ■ The *Wild* Ways of God ■ ■ ■ ■ ■ ■

The *wilderness* and *wild beasts* that Mark mentions in his account of the temptation symbolize the heart of Satan's domain.[7] Which means Jesus didn't do battle with the enemy in a well-lit boxing ring governed by an impartial referee and surrounded by cheering fans eating popcorn. Instead, He bravely marched into the scariest place imaginable, knowing full well someone far worse than Freddy Krueger or a nut job in a hockey mask awaited Him.

A VERY ROUGH TRANSITION

On a flight to Pittsburgh recently, I experienced a new and rather shocking sensation. I was settled in an exit-row middle seat on an oversold flight with lots of folks who were noticeably unhappy about the cramped quarters. I usually avoid middle seats, but the extra legroom made this one more attractive. As we taxied from the gate, I pondered the blessing of being wedged between two polite gentlemen with good hygiene. I was so happy not to be next to someone with a screaming baby or a giant with intrusive elbows. But my delight turned to dismay soon after take-off when I got unbearably hot and started sweating profusely.

At first I wondered if our row was situated above the engine, but when I sneaked a glance to my left and right at my seatmates, they seemed oblivious to the oven underneath us. Both appeared to be comfortably absorbed in their newspapers. Even though they should've been warmer than I was since they were wearing jackets while I was wearing a thin, long-sleeved shirt, neither one had perspiration dripping off his nose. After a few more minutes spent roasting in my own fiery inferno, it finally dawned on me what was actually happening. And thus began my sudden and uncomfortable transition into middle age!

However, as rude awakenings go, mine had nothing on Jesus's sudden transition from the scene of His baptism to His battle with Satan:

> At that time Jesus came from the town of Nazareth in Galilee
> and was baptized by John in the Jordan River. Immediately, as
> Jesus was coming up out of the water, he saw heaven open.
> The Holy Spirit came down on him like a dove, and a voice
> came from heaven: "You are my Son, whom I love, and I am
> very pleased with you."

Then the Spirit sent Jesus into the desert. He was in the desert forty days and was tempted by Satan. He was with the wild animals, and the angels came and took care of him. *Mark 1:9–13, NCV*

Most Bibles include a break—often a new paragraph or heading—after John's baptism of Jesus in the Jordan River, which suggests a transitional pause between the Holy Spirit descending on Him like a dove and the Holy Spirit banishing Him to the desert. But ancient manuscripts don't include such literary niceties. Jesus went directly from that heart-lifting swim to a heart-wrenching assault.

Mark Galli, the managing editor of *Christianity Today,* explains the abrupt shift like this:

This is the same Spirit who just a moment earlier was the visible image of the Father's love, sent by the Father to show Jesus he is beloved, pleasing, a splendor to behold, symbolizing the pristine beginning of something wonderfully new. Now this Spirit drives the beloved Son into the desert. Literally, in the Greek in which this was written, Jesus is "cast out" from the warmth of home and friends, from the comforts of town and village. He is denied even moral and spiritual support—the Torah, the synagogue, the wisdom of the town elders, even, it seems, the comfort of the heavenly Father's presence. Jesus is driven into the wilderness, deserted by love, to face a hostile adversary alone.[8]

I don't know too many people who could handle such an abrupt shift in circumstances—from community to isolation; from adoration to abandonment. Most of us would end up depressed in bed or drunk in a bar. But Jesus isn't like most people, and He didn't come anywhere close to coming unhinged. He hung *tough emotionally.*

MENTAL METTLE

My friend and sometimes trainer Dominick DiVito is an imposing Italian guy. He's an expert in martial arts, has worked in security for several celebrities, and has been featured as a self-defense specialist on television shows such as *Fight Science* on the National Geographic Channel. He could definitely best pretty much anybody in a brawl. Yet Dom avoids fisticuffs the way I avoid men wearing pinkie rings and too much cologne. He insists it takes more strength to ignore some punk spoiling for a fight than it does to knock him out.

Jesus displayed a similar kind of restraint when the devil came swaggering by, looking to spar:

> Then the Spirit led Jesus into the desert to be tempted by the devil. Jesus fasted for forty days and nights. After this, he was very hungry. The devil came to Jesus to tempt him, saying, "If you are the Son of God, tell these rocks to become bread."
>
> Jesus answered, "It is written in the Scriptures, 'A person lives not on bread alone, but by everything God says.' "
> *Matthew 4:1–4, NCV*

Satan's first swing was taunting Jesus—who hadn't eaten in forty days—to turn some nearby stones into bread. Jesus ducked and said, "The Living Word is tastier than a loaf of bread."

Then the devil led Jesus to the holy city of Jerusalem and put
him on a high place of the Temple. The devil said, "If you are the
Son of God, jump down, because it is written in the Scriptures:
    'He has put his angels in charge of you.
        They will catch you in their hands
    so that you will not hit your foot on a rock.' "
Jesus answered him, "It also says in the Scriptures, 'Do
not test the Lord your God.' " *Matthew 4:5–7,* NCV

In the second temptation we see the devil attempting to sucker-punch
our Savior with a base-jumping dare. Jesus feigned deftly by reminding
the slithery liar that His Dad didn't want Him to join the circus.

Then the devil led Jesus to the top of a very high mountain
and showed him all the kingdoms of the world and all their
splendor. The devil said, "If you will bow down and worship
me, I will give you all these things."
    Jesus said to the devil, "Go away from me, Satan! It is
written in the Scriptures, 'You must worship the Lord your
God and serve only him.' " *Matthew 4:8–10,* NCV

Lastly, Lucifer went for the knockout by telling Jesus He could rule
the world if He'd just slip on a "Satan's Team" jersey. But Jesus put up a
hand and stopped the accuser's fist in midswing. Then He calmly forced
the enemy's trembling arm down while saying firmly, "Leave Me alone,
loser. Jehovah's jersey is the only one I'm interested in wearing."

So the devil left Jesus, and angels came and took care of him.
Matthew 4:11, NCV

By dodging all three temptations, our Redeemer refused to serve Himself, defy the Father, or redirect His worship. It was a definitive setback for evil and a rousing triumph for good. Only a *mentally tough* warrior could've made that happen.

The *Wild* Ways of God

The gospel of Matthew reveals that our untamed Savior definitely wasn't afraid of heights, because several key moments in His life and ministry take place on mountaintops: His third round during the temptation bout with Satan took place on a *high* mountain, His first sermon took place on a mountain, the transfiguration took place on a *high* mountain, and the last literal words He spoke (known as the "Great Commission") were also preached from a mountain peak.[9]

TOUGH LOVE, TENDER MERCIES

Looking back on the day my dad rescued me from an angry bull, I've come to understand why it was so significant. It wasn't simply that Dad was tough; it was how he exerted his toughness on my behalf. And to a little girl who sometimes wondered how her daddy could walk away into the arms of another family yet still love her, it proved to me that he did. The fact that he was willing to step in front of a moving freight train with horns to protect me meant he must really, really love me.

Which is also why the fierce tenacity of Jesus is so significant. He went toe-to-toe with Lucifer because He knew our eternity was at stake, and He was wildly determined to protect us from Satan's schemes to rob us of salvation, to kill our hope, and to destroy our lives. And that ferocity wasn't a one-time demonstration during His time on earth either. Even now our Savior is standing at the right hand of God the Father, interceding on our behalf and making sure that nothing—absolutely nothing—threatens our relationship with Him.[10]

Jesus is physically, emotionally, and mentally willing and able to fight dangerous beasts, and He does so *on our behalf.* The fact that He is as tough as He is tender is all the more proof that He really, really loves us.

We need an untamed *Savior because...* only a *wildly tough* Redeemer can free us from our fears by committing Himself to protect us, no matter what the cost.

■ ■ Living and Loving with Abandon ■ ■

1. In what ways does your mental image of Jesus change when you picture Him as a stonemason instead of a carpenter?

2. Reread about Jesus's abrupt transition from His baptism to the desert in Mark 1:9–13. What sudden transition has left you reeling recently?

3. Read Hebrews 12:1–2 and Matthew 27:27–31. What other words would you use to describe the way Jesus "endured the cross" on our behalf?

4. Read Hebrews 12:3. Whom do you most admire in your circle of friends because of the way his or her hope in Christ hasn't dimmed in spite of persecution or adversity? How can you tell that person's hope is alive?

5. Read Genesis 3:1–7 and Luke 4:1–13. What similarities do you see between how Satan tempted Adam and Eve in the Garden of Eden and how he tempted Jesus in the

wilderness? How would you contrast the outcomes of these two events?

6. Read John 16:33 and Romans 6:1–4. Our Savior triumphed over Satan and overcame the world. Because the same Spirit who raised Him from the dead now lives in us, what or who can truly defeat us? How can this truth help shape your perspective in the trial that is currently testing your mettle to the max and causing you to question how you'll survive?

5

Simply Irresistible

Our Savior Is *Wildly* Compelling

His character enchants, subdues, overwhelms—
and with the irresistible impulse of its own sacred
attraction it draws your spirit right up to Him.

—CHARLES SPURGEON

■ ■ ■ ■ ■ ■

Today was a sunny, seventy-degree day, and because the weather in Tennessee has mirrored Minnesota for the past few weeks, I felt compelled to go outside and revel in the warmth. I gleefully shut down the computer, threw on some shorts, and whistled for my dogs—Dottie and Harley—because I knew they'd enjoy a romp through the woods too. Sure enough, as soon as they saw me reach for the leash, they nearly levitated with enthusiasm.

When we got to the trailhead, I fastened them both to a coupler (a nylon strap with collar clips on either end and a metal ring in the middle, thereby allowing one leash to connect two dogs) and was immediately wrenched forward by fifty-some combined pounds of hyperhound. After the initial jerk, I enjoyed jogging behind my furry friends and found myself amused by their disparity.

Harley is a long-legged Jack Russell terrier—sleek and fast. Dottie is a short-legged Jack and looks like a balloon with paws—round and dawdling. Harley ran effortlessly over the rocky path while Dottie huffed and puffed and stumbled along. It was like watching a gazelle and a walrus compete in a three-legged race! But while Dottie's clumsiness slowed him down, pulled him off balance, and even got them tangled around a tree trunk at one point, Harley never growled or barked at her. In fact, he actually licked her encouragingly a few times along the way as if to say, "Don't worry, Dottie. I think chunky chicks are hot!"

I couldn't help pondering how my dogs' odd-couple pairing is a lot like Jesus and His disciples. After John baptized Jesus in the Jordan to officially kick off His public ministry and Jesus endured that title bout with Satan in the wilderness to prepare for what lay ahead, it was time to pick some teammates. And since He had all of humanity to choose from, you'd think Jesus would've chosen the best and the brightest to join His squad. That He would've loitered around campuses like Oxford and Harvard to recruit brilliant academic types, strolled the halls of the Mayo Clinic to find a team physician, interviewed soldiers to enlist brave idealists for the gospel campaign, and maybe even visited tough-guy competitions to hire a couple of brawlers to protect Him from His enemies.

> If you got to choose a team of people to walk through the rest of life with, what are the main qualities you'd want in your teammates?

Yet instead of handpicking a dream team, Jesus willingly harnessed Himself to twelve mostly uneducated, unsophisticated men. They were the type of ruffians who would argue among themselves like contestants on *Survivor* and slice off a stranger's ear with a sword. Frankly, they were by and large such a coarse crew it's a wonder they were willing to leave their jobs to work with the Messiah in full-time ministry for no pay.

But then again, the Man they followed—the same One who beckons us into untamed faith—was *wildly compelling.*

A Team Made Up Entirely of Walk-Ons

I've been on lots of organized teams—volleyball, tennis, track, student government, basketball, and Kappa Delta sorority, to name a few. Each required new recruits to endure a tryout or election process whereby those who performed well made the cut while the less adept were excluded. When I was in elementary school, we even employed a mandatory initiation process to determine who could become part of the disorganized gang (think Little Rascals, not Crips and Bloods) that ruled our neighborhood.

Patty Brooks and I were two of the original members of the close-knit community of kids who lived on Valencia Avenue and played freeze tag and hide-and-seek or chased the mosquito truck on our bikes most every summer night. And being savvy nine-year-olds, we realized we needed a system by which to ostracize sissies or tattletales who could potentially spoil our no-parents-allowed fun. So we created an obstacle course of tree climbing, fence walking (where the gang wannabe had to walk a predetermined distance on a wobbly chain-link fence), and timed running. If—and only if—a boy or girl was able to pass the skills tests without whining was that individual granted membership in our motley crew.

Astonishingly, that Valencia Avenue band of barefoot hooligans was tougher on new recruits than Jesus was. He didn't make His disciples sprint to the end of the block and back while He counted, "One Mississippi, two Mississippi, three Mississippi," and He didn't demand an initiation fee so He could buy a Bomb Pop from the ice-cream-truck man. Nor did Jesus ask them to take an entrance exam, get a physical, or write an essay. He didn't even ask for references. Our Savior simply walked up to a group of scruffy fishermen Johnny B had introduced Him to earlier[1] and said, "Follow me":

Passing along the beach of Lake Galilee, he saw Simon and
his brother Andrew net-fishing. Fishing was their regular
work. Jesus said to them, "Come with me. I'll make a new
kind of fisherman out of you. I'll show you how to catch men
and women instead of perch and bass." They didn't ask questions. They dropped their nets and followed.

A dozen yards or so down the beach, he saw the brothers
James and John, Zebedee's sons. They were in the boat,
mending their fishnets. Right off, he made the same offer.
Immediately, they left their father Zebedee, the boat, and the
hired hands, and followed. *Mark 1:16–20, MSG*

A little while later Jesus was strolling along the shore of Galilee
again, perhaps trying to relax and cool off after being crammed in a
claustrophobic home church, healing a paralytic who literally dropped
in, and then being accused of blasphemy by a bunch of judgmental
jerks.[2] When He came upon an IRS agent named Levi sitting in a
sandy cubicle and playing solitaire, Jesus didn't hesitate to issue another
invitation:

Then Jesus went out to the lakeshore again and taught the
crowds that were coming to him. As he walked along, he saw
Levi son of Alphaeus sitting at his tax collector's booth. "Follow me and be my disciple," Jesus said to him. So Levi got up
and followed him. *Mark 2:13–14, NLT*

The gospel writer Mark helpfully tallies up the whole dirty dozen
Jesus called to follow Him:

These are the twelve men he chose: Simon (Jesus named him Peter), James and John, the sons of Zebedee (Jesus named them Boanerges, which means "Sons of Thunder"), Andrew, Philip, Bartholomew, Matthew, Thomas, James the son of Alphaeus, Thaddaeus, Simon the Zealot, and Judas Iscariot, who later turned against Jesus. *Mark 3:16–19, NCV*

The bottom line on Jesus's homeboys is that…

- Simon, also called Peter, was a strong-willed outdoorsman;
- James and John were fishermen with fiery personalities;
- Andrew was also a fisherman and a social networker who introduced his big brother Pete to Jesus;
- Philip was a pragmatic bean counter;
- Bartholomew, also called Nathanael, was a very direct guy who made it clear he didn't think anything good—much less the Messiah—could come out of dinky Nazareth…that is, until he met Jesus;
- Matthew, also called Levi, had a soft spot for Armani suits and five-star restaurants;
- Thomas, also called the "Twin," was a worrywart;
- James the son of Alphaeus, also called James the younger, was evidently a shy guy, because he's rarely mentioned again in the Gospels;
- Thaddaeus, also called the good Judas, was a salesman at heart;
- Simon the Zealot was a Jewish idealist whose nostrils flared when anyone slandered Israel or extolled the virtues of Rome; and

- Judas Iscariot was the infamous traitor who betrayed Jesus for cold, hard cash.[3]

The disciples certainly weren't statesmen or scholars, but they *were* street-smart. As fishermen, Peter, Andrew, James, and John had learned how to navigate their boats by the moon and stars because they fished at night. As a tax collector, Matthew had figured out how to cook the books without being busted for embezzling. And as an enemy of the state, Simon the Zealot had managed to stay one step ahead of Roman authorities.

These weren't the kind of men who were easily impressed or intimidated. Yet without hesitation they abandoned their livelihoods and followed Jesus. Doesn't that make you wonder what kind of authority emanated from our Savior?

■ ■ ■ ■ ■ ■ The *Wild* Ways of God ■ ■ ■ ■ ■ ■

The fact that Jesus chose exactly twelve disciples is likely a New Testament nod to the twelve tribes and twelve patriarchs of ancient Israel.[4]

THE PERFECT BLEND OF OIL AND WATER

Not only was Jesus's choice of disciples unorthodox and His authorization process nonexistent, but the personalities He merged together were outwardly irreconcilable. For instance, Peter was the optimistic Energizer Bunny type:

Peter broke in, "Even if everyone else falls to pieces on account of you, I won't." *Matthew 26:33,* MSG

While Thomas was more of a pessimistic Eeyore, as demonstrated by his comment upon learning that Lazarus had died:

> That's when Thomas, the one called the Twin, said to his companions, "Come along. We might as well die with him."
> *John 11:16, MSG*

Then there's Simon the seething Zealot and Matthew the extortionist.

Simon was a revolutionary who bitterly resented Rome's authority over Israel and the resulting anti-Semitism and oppressive taxation. In fact, his hatred of Rome was so intense that, prior to becoming Jesus's disciple, he'd been a card-carrying member of the Zealots, an organization that endorsed Al Qaeda–like violence in their quest to overthrow Rome. So naturally Jesus plopped him nose to nose with Matthew, who'd collaborated with Rome by collecting tariffs on goods being imported and exported from Israel!

Furthermore, tax collectors (also called "publicans," because they gathered public revenue on behalf of the government) were reviled for charging whatever the market would bear and then skimming off the top before turning the coffers over to Rome. Which meant Matthew had built his bank account on the backs of his own countrymen. His Mercedes and fancy Mediterranean home came at the expense of his hard-working Jewish neighbors.

You'd be hard-pressed to find two people more philosophically opposed than Simon and Matt. Putting them together was like pairing Robert E. Lee with Ulysses S. Grant. Or a Florida football fan with a Florida State football fan. Or Jennifer Aniston with Angelina Jolie. Few people would've bet on the union—except perhaps to wager they'd get into fisticuffs within two weeks of joining the same team! Yet those two opposites, as well as the rest of the disciples (with the notable exception of Judas Iscariot), forged a brotherly bond and became a cohesive group of missionaries. Their unlikely solidarity could have happened only as a result of Jesus's compelling leadership!

■ ■ ■ ■ ■ ■ The *Wild* Ways of God ■ ■ ■ ■ ■ ■

According to church tradition, ten disciples died a martyr's death for the cause of Christ. James was put to death by the sword—likely beheaded (Acts 12:2)—and legend has it that Peter was crucified upside down in the shape of an X, an event Jesus prophesied in John 21:18. These men's willingness to die horrible deaths proves they found Jesus just as compelling after His death and resurrection as they did when He was their incarnate leader.

AN OFFER THEY COULDN'T REFUSE

Several years ago I answered a persistent knock at my door to find two polite young men dressed in white shirts, dark pants, and clip-on ties standing on the porch. They also wore nervous smiles, and one of them asked if they could have a few moments of my time to share a life-changing opportunity. It was obvious they were selling something, and I really didn't feel like hearing their pitch, but it was one of those ninety-degree, 95-percent-humidity summer days, and I felt sorry for them, so I invited them into the living room.

The minute they sat down, their well-rehearsed spiel touting Mormonism tumbled out. I listened intently until the biggest talker took a breath, then I interjected the fact that I was a committed Christian. I explained that, while I respected their belief system and had actually studied the writings of Joseph Smith, I wasn't interested in becoming a Mormon convert, because my hope and faith are in Jesus Christ alone. My confession flustered them for a few seconds, but they regrouped and began a coordinated effort to encourage me to see the flaws in Christianity and switch my allegiance to the Church of Latter-day Saints.

It took a while to convince those two well-intentioned boys that I wasn't going to follow them. First of all, their religion is riddled with historical and theological holes. Second, as misguided, barely-out-of-high-school proselytizers, they didn't have any authority over me. Neither their truth claims nor their personal convictions were persuasive enough for me to buy what they were selling.

Their anxious and aggressive efforts stood in stark contrast to Jesus's confident directive. Can you imagine some guy striding up while you're busy—pecking away on a laptop or putting dirty laundry into the washing machine or mending your fishing net—and saying, "Leave that and come away with me"? More important, can you imagine actually abandoning whatever it is you were doing and traipsing off after the stranger without so much as a brochure detailing his plans or 401(k) options?

I've heard the story of the calling of disciples preached many times but until recently had never truly considered how utterly compelling Jesus must've been for those guys to sacrifice everything—family, friends, comfortable housing, jobs, romantic interests—and follow Him. Jesus's costly command illustrates His divinity, because only the God who created us can rightfully demand our very lives. And their immediate obedience underscores the undeniable influence and authority Christ must have exuded.

Jesus wasn't a twenty-something hawking faulty religion or some smarmy guy in a cheap suit peddling encyclopedias. He is the Lion of Judah, and when He roared, "Follow me," Peter, James, John, Andrew, Philip, Bartholomew, Matthew, Thomas, Jimmy, Thaddaeus, Simon, and Judas essentially sprinted toward Him in response. Soon afterward they got to watch hordes of others hustle toward Jesus too:

And great crowds followed him from Galilee and the Decapolis, and from Jerusalem and Judea, and from beyond the Jordan. *Matthew 4:25*

Again Jesus began teaching by the lake. A great crowd gathered around him, so he sat down in a boat near the shore. All the people stayed on the shore close to the water. *Mark 4:1, NCV*

The next day, when they came down from the mountain, a large crowd met him. *Luke 9:37, NIV*

When Jesus looked out and saw that a large crowd had arrived, he said to Philip, "Where can we buy bread to feed these people?" *John 6:5, MSG*

What kind of Man is so wildly compelling that He instantly gains the allegiance of twelve tough guys, captures the rapt attention of audiences willing to forgo food to listen to Him teach for hours on end, and causes traffic jams because swarms of admirers follow Him wherever He goes? The best answer I've heard to this question was preached by Charles

Haddon Spurgeon in 1860: "I *must* love You. It is *impossible* for me to resist it—that thought that You love *me* has compelled my soul to love You."⁵ Of course, the premise of Dr. Spurgeon's message comes from something one of those unruly disciples wrote almost two thousand years earlier:

We love because he first loved us. *1 John 4:19, NIV*

My mom is old-fashioned when it comes to romance. Her basic philosophy is, "Women shouldn't initiate with men. If you make them pursue you at the beginning, they'll chase you till the end." Of course, now that I'm closing in on an AARP membership and still single, I tease her about how it might've benefited me to take a little initiative! Fortunately for us, unlike the shy suitors in my dating history, our Savior pursues us to the extreme. He takes the lead in loving us. He *calls* us into relationship with Him.

People weren't compelled to follow Jesus because He was a megawatt superstar who filled stadiums, wrote bestsellers, and was flanked by a posse of security guys. The disciples and the crowds drew close mainly because they sensed He *cared* about them. Jesus won their hearts by declaring and demonstrating His affection first. And the more I contemplate His passionate quest for my own heart—the way He winks at me through brilliant sunrises, provides enough money to pay the bills, and serenades me with crickets at night—the more I'm compelled to run after Him the way I did after Stan in the Sanford Christmas parade!

I am growing ever more smitten with the One who is so obviously taken with me. How about you?

We need an untamed *Savior because...*
only a *wildly compelling* Jesus frees our hearts to race
toward Him when He calls.

▪ ▪ Living and Loving with Abandon ▪ ▪

1. Which one of the twelve disciples do you most identify with, and
   why?

2. When was the first time you felt compelled by Jesus calling you to
   follow Him? What was your response?

3. Read Matthew 8:18–22. What would be the most difficult thing
   or relationship for you to give up if you, like the disciples, literally
   left everything in order to follow a flesh-and-blood Jesus?

4. Read Matthew 14:1–14. Because of the insistency of the crowds following Him, Jesus didn't have the time or privacy to grieve John the Baptist's death. Yet instead of getting irritated, He had compassion on the people. When has a Christian leader (maybe a pastor or Bible teacher) shown you compassion when he or she could've legitimately dismissed you as clingy or exasperating?

5. Read Matthew 14:22–33. Once he realized Jesus wasn't a ghost, Peter was so compelled by His majesty that he attempted to walk on water toward the Lord! What's the craziest thing you've done lately in an effort to get as close to Jesus as you possibly can?

6. Read John 13:21–25 and John 21:20. Both of these passages refer to an intimate moment John shared with Jesus during the Last Supper, when he literally leaned against the Messiah's chest. Describe a moment when you felt as if you were being held by Jesus.

6

A Little Pink
in the Party

Our Savior Is *Wildly* Pro-Women

The beloved physician's book has been called The
Gospel of Womanhood, for the Savior's tender and
profound regard for women comes to the fore in this
Gospel more clearly than in any other.

—WILLIAM HENDRIKSEN

You know how it says "Objects in mirror are closer than they appear" on the side-view mirror of your car? Well, I need to begin this chapter with a similar disclaimer: my stepfather is about to appear more chauvinistic than I wish he'd been. I should also note that Alzheimer's now muddles his once-brilliant mind, and he can no longer read or comprehend what I'm about to disclose. Furthermore, I do love him and don't want to disparage him. I just wish I'd talked to him about some of this stuff when he could understand it.

John Angel seemed bigger than life to me when he and Mom got married. He had broad shoulders, wavy salt-and-pepper hair, piercing blue eyes, and a booming laugh. He used to tell me to bend my arms and keep my fists tight to my side, then he'd put his hands under my elbows and hoist me over his head. As a six-year-old who desperately longed for a dad's consistent affection, I thought John was the bomb! He taught me to cast a rod and reel, to read voraciously, to execute an elegant swan dive, to sand with the grain of wood, and to look people in the eyes when speaking to them.

But he also trained me to think men were more important than women.

My first lesson in my limitations as a female took place at the breakfast table soon after he became my stepfather. As I reached for a piece of bacon, he popped my hand with his butter knife, saying, "Girls shouldn't eat bacon, or they'll get fat."

I quickly found out I'd better not ask for second helpings of anything other than salad, much less pilfer from his Oreo stash, because according to John, "Men aren't attracted to big women." My final exam in gender inequity took place about ten years later when he said he wouldn't spend one dime on my college tuition because most women who went to college just got married and had babies and never ended up using their degrees anyway. Although he worked as a teacher, principal, and school superintendent throughout his career, he didn't think I needed to be educated past high school.

> Describe a time when you picked up the
> message that women are somehow
> less valuable than men.

I don't remember making a conscious decision to believe that boys are more valuable than girls, but until just a few years ago, that distorted assumption was etched into the deepest grooves of my heart. Unfortunately, quite a few Christian men along the way have reinforced John's twisted logic. One guy actually told me the reason my salary was so much lower than my less-experienced male counterparts was because God *wanted* them to earn more! Then he observed that if I had more of the gentle and quiet spirit God commands of women, I wouldn't be bothered by our disparity in pay. Looking back, I recognize his reasoning was self-serving, but at the time it sounded plausible. Even though his chauvinistic diatribe hurt my feelings and ignited a firestorm of guilt about my lack of submission, I assumed he was right about God preferring men over women.

Given all the "boys rule" messages that have assaulted my heart over the years, it's been a wonderfully liberating surprise to learn that Jesus is *wildly pro-women.*

HOPE BEYOND COOKING AND CLEANING

One of my favorite magazines is *Real Simple.* When I retrieve it from the mailbox every month, the first section I flip to is Solutions, where they write about new uses for old things. Some of the recent *aha* applications I've read about are using a melon baller to scoop the seeds out of a tomato, using a curtain rod in a kitchen drawer to corral pot lids, using paint chips as place cards (simply fold two colors, print a name on one side, and, presto, your guests will know where to sit at the dinner table), and finally using Play-Doh to hold lit sparklers—that way kids can hold on to the plastic container instead of the metal wand, and their sticky hands won't get burned by errant sparks.[1] Who would've thought colored dough had the potential to shield minipyromaniacs from bodily harm? Your deck might go up in flames, but Junior will be blister free!

When Jesus added women to His entourage, it provided an *aha* moment for an entire culture. And it was profoundly more significant than just finding a new use for some old gadget; it meant people began to regard women as being capable of far more than cleaning house and cooking supper:

Soon afterward he went on through cities and villages, pro-
claiming and bringing the good news of the kingdom of God.
And the twelve were with him, and also some women who
had been healed of evil spirits and infirmities: Mary, called
Magdalene, from whom seven demons had gone out, and
Joanna, the wife of Chuza, Herod's household manager, and
Susanna, and many others, who provided for them out of
their means. *Luke 8:1–3*

Men across Israel cocked their heads sideways, thinking, *Wow, I
didn't realize my daughter had the potential to travel and study and minister with the Messiah!* Women in spiritual leadership was a novel concept
in this patriarchal society where women were typically disregarded as
chattel—as something a man could *own*. And the guys on the local
God Squad didn't try to dissuade the bigotry either; in fact, they fanned
the flames of discrimination. For instance, an ancient rabbinic proverb
declared, "It's better that the Torah be burned than it should be taught
to a woman."[2] Even more disheartening, a common prayer was "Blessed
art thou, O God, who did not make me a woman."[3]

Therefore the description of Jesus's posse as a dozen mistake-prone
men *and* three chicks was a totally radical concept. Radical because in
ancient Jewish culture, women had limited access to education and
generally were restricted to performing domestic duties.[4] By allowing
them to be an integral part of His public ministry, Jesus challenged a
centuries-old paradigm of women being subjugated as second-class
citizens.

In short, the inclusion of women in Jesus's inner circle proves He
considered women *valuable.* He treated them as trusted companions and
worthy ambassadors of the gospel.

■ ■ ■ ■ ■ ■ The *Wild* Ways of God ■ ■ ■ ■ ■ ■

The Bible is filled with awesome examples of our Creator using women to carry out His purposes and even lead His people. One of the best-known cases is that of Deborah, who led the nation of Israel into battle after Barak—Israel's highest-ranking military officer—balked and said he wasn't going anywhere unless she went with him. And the most colorful chick has to be Jael, who drove a tent peg through Sisera's temple (the same wicked warmonger Deborah and Barak fought against) while he was taking a nap.[5] Which just goes to show that being handy with a hammer isn't limited to the males of our species!

MARY, MARY, NOT CONTRARY

My mother didn't allow my sister, brother, and me to watch R-rated movies when we were growing up, and though I viewed a few contraband flicks, I never saw *The Exorcist.* For those of you who also had protective moms, *The Exorcist* was a 1973 horror flick that catapulted little Linda Blair into stardom. Based on clips and parodies I *have* seen, that young actress deserved the recognition because she had to pretend to be possessed by a demon and in one scene reportedly spewed split pea soup to make her exorcism appear more realistic on-screen. As scary as that sounds, Hollywood has nothing on Scripture, because the first member of Jesus's estrogen ensemble had *seven* evil spirits aggravating her before He cast them out!

The Bible doesn't elaborate on how that plethora of creeps plagued Mary Magdalene, but based on other demonic possession accounts, it must have been awful. Matthew describes a boy hurling himself into the fire, Mark describes a man who morphed into a Hulk-like creature, and earlier in Luke there's a poor guy who caused an embarrassing scene with his shouted comments as a result of evil spirits.[6] Clearly when Jesus healed her from a similar affliction, this girl from Magdala (which means "The Tower"[7]) became eternally devoted to Him.

▪ ▪ ▪ ▪ ▪ ▪ ▪ ▪ Did You Know... ▪ ▪ ▪ ▪ ▪ ▪ ▪ ▪

Mary from Magdala is often mistakenly identified as the sinful woman—and sometimes described as a former prostitute—who washed Jesus's feet with her tears and dried them with her hair (Luke 7:36–50). However, there's no evidence for that in Scripture or early church historical texts. This case of mistaken identity is due to people confusing the story of Mary *from Bethany* anointing Jesus's feet (Matthew 26:6–13; Mark 14:3–9; John 12:1–7) with an *unnamed* woman giving Him a footbath in Luke.[8]

In fact, the Gospels reveal that Mary Magdalene did more than traipse along behind Jesus with a video camera and a goofy smile; she was one of the few members of His team who bravely stayed put at the foot of the cross during His torturous death.[9] She then followed His lifeless body all the way to the tomb,[10] and when she returned to that stone crypt to prepare her Lord's body for burial, it was Mary from Magdala who first witnessed that the stone had been rolled away and Jesus was no longer in the grave:

> Early in the morning on the first day of the week, while it was still dark, Mary Magdalene came to the tomb and saw that the stone was moved away from the entrance. She ran at once to Simon Peter and the other disciple, the one Jesus loved, breathlessly panting, "They took the Master from the tomb. We don't know where they've put him."
>
> Peter and the other disciple left immediately for the tomb. They ran, neck and neck. The other disciple got to the tomb first, outrunning Peter. Stooping to look in, he saw the pieces of linen cloth lying there, but he didn't go in. Simon Peter arrived after him, entered the tomb, observed the linen cloths lying there, and the kerchief used to cover his head not lying with the linen cloths but separate, neatly folded by itself. Then the other disciple, the one who had gotten there first, went into the tomb, took one look at the evidence, and believed. No one yet knew from the Scripture that he had to rise from the dead. The disciples then went back home. *John 20:1–10, MSG*

The boys hurried away, anxious to tell others the stone had been rolled away and Jesus's body was no longer in the tomb. But Mary Magdalene stayed behind, too overwhelmed by the turn of events to move.

> But Mary stood outside the tomb weeping. As she wept, she knelt to look into the tomb and saw two angels sitting there, dressed in white, one at the head, the other at the foot of

where Jesus' body had been laid. They said to her, "Woman, why do you weep?"

"They took my Master," she said, "and I don't know where they put him." After she said this, she turned away and saw Jesus standing there. But she didn't recognize him.

Jesus spoke to her, "Woman, why do you weep? Who are you looking for?"

She, thinking that he was the gardener, said, "Mister, if you took him, tell me where you put him so I can care for him." *John 20:11–15, MSG*

Mary probably mistook Jesus for the gardener because the sun wasn't completely up yet, and it was hard to see clearly in the shadows. But I still would've loved to see Jesus's expression in that moment. I imagine Him suppressing a grin!

Jesus said, "Mary."

Turning to face him, she said in Hebrew, "Rabboni!" meaning "Teacher!"

Jesus said, "Don't cling to me, for I have not yet ascended to the Father. Go to my brothers and tell them, 'I ascend to my Father and your Father, my God and your God.'"

Mary Magdalene went, telling the news to the disciples: "I saw the Master!" And she told them everything he said to her. *John 20:16–18, MSG*

Mary's emotional state immediately changed from profound grief to utter delight. Her gulping sobs turned into a cascade of excited giggles.

And after witnessing the risen Christ—her hero, now glorified—she couldn't wait to shout, "I saw the Lord!" to the disciples!

Pastor and author John Ortberg calls Jesus's resurrection "the fulcrum of the Christian faith."[11] In other words, our entire belief system hinges on Easter—on the truth that our Savior didn't stay dead. While I wholeheartedly agree with that theological assessment, I've recently begun to appreciate another facet of the resurrection story—certainly not as important as the promise of salvation and eternal life, which is the result of Jesus's conquering sin and death, but significant nonetheless: that God chose to entrust the initial evidence to a woman.

Our Creator Redeemer is a God of details—He put stripes on zebras and gave atoms their nucleus—so you can bet *everything* about that first Easter week was preordained, from the placement of the cross to the borrowed tomb. Additionally, it would have made more sense to have a man as the first witness of the resurrection because it was assumed they made more reliable witnesses. Women weren't even allowed to participate in the legal system during the time of Christ. Yet our God chose a *woman* for what could be accurately described as the most important job in history.

Mary Magdalene's slender shoulders are the ones on which the testimony of His risenness rests. Pretty cool, huh?

SHE COULD BRING HOME THE BACON AND FRY IT UP IN A PAN

With all my huffing and puffing about the importance of valuing men and women equally, I have to confess there's one area where I'm a giant hypocrite, and that's the area of money. Perhaps it's because I was steeped in the traditionalism of the Deep South, or maybe it's because I heard

Mom say, "A man who doesn't provide for his family is worse than an infidel" (1 Timothy 5:8, Patti's translation) when my dad skipped on child-support payments.

Whatever the reason, I like it when men pick up the check. It somehow seems less manly to me when a guy is slow to reach for his wallet. I know it's terribly sexist and selfish, and I'm praying about it, but a faint Zsa Zsa Gabor voice whispers in my brain, *You should marry a rich man instead of a poor one so you can fritter away your cash on new shoes, and he can spring for the new roof!*

Jesus didn't have the same financial misconceptions; He was fine going Dutch:

> He continued according to plan, traveled to town after town, village after village, preaching God's kingdom, spreading the Message. The Twelve were with him. There were also some women in their company who had been healed of various evil afflictions and illnesses: Mary, the one called Magdalene, from whom seven demons had gone out; Joanna, wife of Chuza, Herod's manager; and Susanna—*along with many others who used their considerable means to provide for the company. Luke 8:1–3,* MSG, *emphasis added*

Evidently, these ladies were loaded. Or at least sufficiently well off to help pay the expenses incurred on all those mission trips. Plus, the phrase "many others" and the pronoun "who" are both feminine in the original Greek manuscripts of Luke,[12] which means Mary, Joanna, and Susanna had girlfriends who supported Jesus's ministry as well. Picture a first-century book club filled with chicks who wrote checks! Which also means Jesus didn't view women as weak and dependent. When they pulled out their purses, He didn't patronize them and say, "Put that away. You girls save your money, because there's a Nordstrom in the next town!" Instead, He humbly allowed them to invest in His life's work. He treated them with dignity.

■ ■ ■ ■ ■ ■ The *Wild* Ways of God ■ ■ ■ ■ ■ ■

> Luke, a physician and close friend of the apostle Paul, is probably the only non-Jewish person to write Holy Scripture.[13] (He wrote both Luke and Acts, which are essentially parts 1 and 2 of his gospel—or good news—story.) And his inclusion in the biblical canon (books considered authoritative as Scripture) is a clear reflection of God's plan to make His grace accessible to people from every tribe, tongue, and nation!

I Now Pronounce You Important

I don't remember where I first heard it, but I've never forgotten the story about the man and the wheelbarrow.[14]

Legend has it there was an elderly man who rolled a wheelbarrow through a border checkpoint to get from where he worked back to his home every night. The guards at the checkpoint levied a tax on anything of value passing through and were convinced he was smuggling goods in his wheelbarrow. So they stopped him each time and pawed through whatever he was carrying—dirt, rocks, or straw—but never could find anything to confiscate. This went on for years, until the old gentleman retired. It was then he moved away and wrote the guards a departing note explaining he'd been smuggling wheelbarrows the entire time!

Joanna must've been as wily as that wheelbarrow smuggler, because her spouse, Chuza ("Cuza" in some translations), was the right-hand man to Herod Antipas. You'll remember that Herod Antipas was the womanizer who had John the Baptist murdered.[15] Plus, his father—Herod the Great—was the megalomaniac who schemed to have Jesus killed when He was a baby.[16] Which means Joanna's missionary work with the Messiah was going on right under the enemy's nose. It's like one of the crazy espionage coups from my favorite televisions series, *24*! Can you imagine how interesting Joanna and Chuza's pillow talk was? Can you imagine how much courage it took to maintain an alliance with Jesus when her husband's boss—a very powerful and jealous man—was His archrival? Once again, Jesus delegated a very important assignment to a *woman*.

Largely due to some complex passages that occur later in the New Testament (namely Ephesians 5:22–24; Colossians 3:18; 1 Timothy 2:11–15; and 1 Peter 3:1–6), which can be difficult to understand and apply without a thorough knowledge of ancient cultural practices and tradition, many well-intentioned Christians earnestly believe women *shouldn't* be given important assignments in society, much less the church. And while I don't have the theological acumen to legitimately debate the modern-day application of murky Greek, I firmly believe the inclusiveness demonstrated by Jesus reveals God is *not* a male chauvinist. He may call us to different *functions*—men can't have babies, and most of them can't walk gracefully in four-inch heels either—but in our heavenly Father's loving eyes, men and women have the same *value*.

We don't have to dumb ourselves down to qualify as good Christian girls. We don't have to swallow our dignity and tolerate off-color jokes made at our expense. We don't have to settle for inequitable salaries and somehow believe that's how our Creator prefers it. Nor does biblical submission mean God expects us to endure physical, emotional, or sexual abuse. Instead, our Redeemer wants His precious daughters to be treated with honor, kindness, and respect.

The darling book *Children's Letters to God*—which has sold far more than a million copies—includes this poignant question from a little girl named Sylvia: "Dear God, are boys better than girls? I know you are one, but please try to be fair."[17] Sylvia's question has reverberated in my heart and mind for a long time. But now I know that God is much more than fair. In fact, I think pink is one of His favorite colors!

Which makes me want to put on high heels and go dancing, followed by a midnight trip to Denny's for a side order of bacon.

We need an untamed *Savior because...* only a Jesus who is *wildly pro-women* frees us from laboring under the lie that women are inferior to men.

▪ ▪ Living and Loving with Abandon ▪ ▪

1. Describe a woman you admire for being both feminine and strong. In what ways are you like her? How do you differ from her?

2. Read John 12:1–8. Can you imagine a man honoring Jesus in the same way Mary did? What does this passage reflect about the unique contributions women can bring to worship?

3. Read 1 Timothy 2:11. This verse has often been used to muzzle women, but in light of the ban on formal education for females during Paul's era, do you think it has a more positive application?

4. Read Genesis 2:18–24. How would you define the term "helper" based on sermons you've heard on this passage?

5. Read Psalm 33:20. How does the fact that God is also described as a "helper" (the same Hebrew word is used for "helper" in

Genesis 2:18 and "help" in Psalm 33:20[18]) affect the definition you gave in answer to question 4? Why do you think *helper* is so often translated as a subservient role?

6. Read Isaiah 54:5 and Revelation 21:1–2. The metaphor of marriage is often used to describe our relationship with God, with redeemed sinners being described as the bride. How would you explain that concept if you had the privilege of teaching Sunday school to a group of little boys?

G eorge Herman Ruth Jr. was born on February 6, 1895. His parents, Kate and George Sr., lived in a rough Baltimore neighborhood known as Pigtown and made a living running bars and selling lightning rods. George's early childhood was hard; only one sister out of seven siblings survived past infancy, and his mother suffered from tuberculosis, which ultimately took her life when he was a teenager. When he was only seven years old, his dad sent him to St. Mary's Industrial School for Boys and signed custody over to the Catholic missionaries who ran the school. It was there George Jr. learned how to play a game called baseball.

When he was nineteen years old, the owner and manager of the Baltimore Orioles, Jack Dunn, signed him to a $250-a-month contract. Since George was technically under age, Dunn also had to become his legal guardian. That fact, coupled with his boyish face, is why the other players nicknamed him "Jack's newest babe," which was quickly shortened to just plain "Babe." Five months later he was traded to the Boston Red Sox, and a few seasons after that, he was traded to the then-struggling

New York Yankees. (The entrepreneurial, theater-loving owner of the Red Sox sold him to finance a Broadway play.[1]) While wearing Yankee pinstripes, Babe Ruth became one of the greatest hitters in baseball history. He was also one of its most confident sluggers.

One of his most celebrated moments occurred during game three of the 1932 World Series. The Yankees were playing the Chicago Cubs at Wrigley Field in Chicago. Because Babe was considered the best player in professional ball at the time, he was naturally a target for the spirited Cubs fans, who were riding a two-games-to-none lead. He and his wife, Helen, were reportedly spit on when they came and went from their hotel, and he was booed when he came on the field. The jeering got meaner still after he hit a three-run homer off pitcher Charlie Root in the first inning. When he got up to bat in the fifth inning, both the Chicago fans and players were ruthless in their provocation.

The nuances of *why* what happened next have been widely debated (some think he was gesturing toward a sick boy to whom he'd promised to hit a home run, and some think his index finger was directed at Charlie Root), but *what* he did was clearly captured on film. After not swinging at two called strikes, Babe Ruth pointed toward center field and hit a home run off the next pitch exactly where he had just pointed! Babe's self-assured "called shot" silenced the rowdy Cub fans for a moment and cemented him in sports history forever.

> How do you tend to project a sense
> of calm assurance when you're in
> an unfriendly environment?

Lots of folks surrounding Jesus were less than encouraging. Jewish religious leaders wondered out loud if He was the devil. Roman politicians branded Him a rabble-rouser. Sometimes even His disciples looked at Him as if He were a few sandwiches short of a picnic. But in spite of the jeers, Jesus didn't waver in the job God gave Him.

Even more so than the Sultan of Swat, Jesus was *wildly confident* in His calling.

LOCAL BOY MAKES GOOD

When Jesus "called His shot," He wasn't at an away stadium but on His home field of Nazareth. It was where He had learned to read and write and had studied the Torah. It was where He'd socialized from the time He was a toddler until He was thirty years old. Kind of like in *Cheers,* it was the one place where everybody knew His name:

And he came to Nazareth, where he had been brought up.
And as was his custom, he went to the synagogue on the
Sabbath day, and he stood up to read. *Luke 4:16*

Initially the Nazareth crowd was supportive. They were probably packed into that small synagogue like sardines, curiously anticipating what Joe and Mary's son had to say. I imagine some of the women bragging to each other about how Jesus used to play with their kids when He was little. But when the Torah scroll was handed to Jesus, the chatting stopped, and every face turned toward Him expectantly.

One of my favorite gospel commentators, William Hendriksen, describes the scene like this:

All is quiet, so quiet that one can hear a feather drop. Every eye
is fixed on Jesus. He opens his mouth. He begins his address.

Does he start out by reminding the audience of the golden days, now gone forever, when Jehovah stretched out his mighty arm and performed miracles on earth? He does not. Does he begin by entertaining his listeners with bright promises pertaining to the future? Not that either.[2]

Right when Jesus has the audience in the palm of His hand, He points to center field:

And the scroll of the prophet Isaiah was given to him. He unrolled the scroll and found the place where it was written,

> "The Spirit of the Lord is upon me,
>> because he has anointed me
>>> to proclaim good news to the poor.
> He has sent me to proclaim liberty to the captives
>> and recovering of sight to the blind,
>>> to set at liberty those who are oppressed,
> to proclaim the year of the Lord's favor."

And he rolled up the scroll and gave it back to the attendant and sat down. And the eyes of all in the synagogue were fixed on him. And he began to say to them, "Today this Scripture has been fulfilled in your hearing." And all spoke well of him and marveled at the gracious words that were coming from his mouth. And they said, "Is not this Joseph's son?" *Luke 4:17–22*

Wow, that's a pretty confident introduction. No joke or engaging human-interest story. Jesus simply strides up to the pulpit and says, "I'm the man!"

■ ■ ■ ■ ■ ■ ■ The *Wild* Ways of God ■ ■ ■ ■ ■ ■ ■

In the Isaiah passage Jesus quoted from in His home-town synagogue, He stopped at the words "the year of the LORD's favor" (Isaiah 61:2a) and did not read the next line about "the day of vengeance of our God" (Isaiah 61:2b). Christ's intentional omission reveals His understanding of His earthly purpose to save the world instead of condemning it.[3]

CALLING IT LIKE IT IS

Because I don't have kids of my own, it's a treat to borrow my friends' little ones. I love their rapid-fire questions, their enthusiasm for sugar, and their propensity for awe. Plus, I love that you usually know where you stand with children, because they rarely edit what they're thinking before they speak. Well, I *almost* always love that part.

I had a friend's little boy on my hip recently while she was juggling her other offspring. We were standing outside his Sunday school class when another woman walked up with her son and began talking about how great it'd be to get them together for a play date. Even though she knew I wasn't the actual mom, I was proud she would converse with me as if I could be a parent. But my loaner child wrecked the fantasy when he looked hard at her lace-collared preschooler and declared loudly, "I do *not* want to play with him because he is a *sissy!*"

The collective reaction of the people in Nazareth also shifted from polite to offended after Jesus followed up the Torah reading with this oh-so-honest commentary:

> Jesus said to them, "I know that you will tell me the old say-
> ing: 'Doctor, heal yourself.' You want to say, 'We heard about
> the things you did in Capernaum. Do those things here in
> your own town!' " Then Jesus said, "I tell you the truth, a
> prophet is not accepted in his hometown. But I tell you the
> truth, there were many widows in Israel during the time of
> Elijah. It did not rain in Israel for three and one-half years,
> and there was no food anywhere in the whole country. But
> Elijah was sent to none of those widows, only to a widow in
> Zarephath, a town in Sidon. And there were many with skin
> diseases living in Israel during the time of the prophet Elisha.
> But none of them were healed, only Naaman, who was from
> the country of Syria."
>
> When all the people in the synagogue heard these things,
> they became very angry. *Luke 4:23–28, NCV*

Mark further elaborates by exposing the ugly root of their negative response:

> "And where did he get the power to do miracles? He is just
> the carpenter, the son of Mary and the brother of James,
> Joseph, Judas, and Simon. And his sisters are here with us."
> So the people were upset with Jesus. *Mark 6:2–3, NCV*

Jesus's friends and neighbors still thought of Him as the boy next-door. They remembered when He used to race around the village courtyard with the other children, playing tag. They'd watched Him mature from a skinned-knee little guy to a gangly adolescent who worked alongside His dad, Joseph. As time passed and Jesus morphed from skinny teenager to strapping man, they'd wondered which local girl He would end up settling down with. So when He stood up in church that morning to give the devotion, they were glad to see Him. Everybody knew He'd been off doing some kind of missionary work. Some had heard rumors He might have even performed a miracle or two. Several people nudged each other and nodded when He began teaching, thinking, *He must do a lot of public speaking on the road, because he's become an eloquent rabbi. We really should ask him to come back here more often.*

Until it dawned on them Jesus wasn't just talking *about God;* He was declaring Himself to *be God.* Heavens to Betsy! Every good Jew knew the tenets of the Torah; they knew the first commandment Jehovah gave Moses was "You shall have no other gods before me" (Exodus 20:3). They knew Israel's God was a jealous God...that He didn't take kindly to anyone upstaging Him or usurping His glory. Yet here was Jesus—*the handyman's kid*—blaspheming about being sent by God Himself to be the divine Deliverer. Some of them probably started scanning the sky for stray lightning bolts. And some of them definitely started clenching their fists. In fact, this crowd got so angry about Jesus's audacious claim they tried to kill Him:

> Jumping up, they mobbed him and forced him to the edge of
> the hill on which the town was built. They intended to push
> him over the cliff, but he passed right through the crowd and
> went on his way. *Luke 4:29–30, NLT*

The *Wild* Ways of God

Jesus's extreme confidence in His calling was probably partly due to the fact that His birth fulfilled many very specific Old Testament prophecies such as:

- The Messiah would come through the lineage of Abraham. (Genesis 17:7-8; 26:3-4)
- The Messiah would come through the lineage of Isaac. (Genesis 17:19; 21:12; 26:2-4; Deuteronomy 18:15-18)
- The Messiah would come through the lineage of David. (2 Samuel 7:12-13; Isaiah 9:7; Jeremiah 23:5)
- The Messiah would come from the tribe of Judah. (Genesis 49:8-10; Micah 5:2; 2 Samuel 2:4)
- The Messiah would be born of a virgin. (Isaiah 7:13-14)
- The Messiah would be a firstborn son. (Exodus 13:2; Numbers 3:13; 8:17)
- The Messiah would be born in Bethlehem of Judea. (Micah 5:2-5)
- Kings would bring Him gifts and fall down before Him. (Psalm 72:10-11)
- There would be a massacre of children around the time of the Messiah's birth. (Jeremiah 31:15)

This list also gives us solid grounds for putting our faith in Jesus as the Messiah!

It's one thing for strangers or rivals to attempt to push you off a cliff, but it's a whole other deal when you went to elementary school with the guys doing the shoving. That kind of cruelty can break your heart. I wonder what expression our confident yet merciful Savior was wearing when He deftly slipped through their grasp and walked out of Nazareth.

THIS IS WHAT I WAS MADE FOR

You're probably familiar with the pivotal scene in the movie *Chariots of Fire,* in which twenty-two-year-old Eric Liddell explains his passion for running to his disapproving sister, who thought running was a waste of time and was keeping him from the mission field of China. "When I run," he said, "I feel his [referring to God] pleasure." Eric Liddell knew that God had made him fast for a reason, that competing in the 1924 Olympics was his calling.

■ ■ ■ ■ ■ ■ ■ ■ Did You Know… ■ ■ ■ ■ ■ ■ ■ ■

Following the 1924 Olympics (where he won gold and bronze medals), Eric Liddell did go to China to serve as a Christian missionary and ended up being interned at a prison camp during World War II. In the fall of 1944, Winston Churchill was able to negotiate the freedom of some of the prisoners from that camp, including the famous Scottish athlete. But Eric Liddell gave up his place to a pregnant prisoner, and he died a few months later while still incarcerated.

It took me a bit longer to figure out my calling in life. It wasn't that I was lazy or aimless; the value of hard work was preached in our house with more fervor than the ban on bacon. So I got my first official job at fourteen and have made regular contributions to Social Security ever since. But purpose is about much more than a paycheck.

In his book *The Call,* Os Guinness explains it like this:

> After all, work, for most of us, determines a great part of our opportunity for significance and the amount of good we are able to produce in a lifetime. Besides, work takes up so many of our waking hours that our jobs come to define us and give us our identities. We become what we do.
>
> Calling reverses such thinking. A sense of calling should precede a choice of job and career, and the main way to discover calling is along the line of what we are each created and gifted to be. Instead of, "You are what you do," calling says: "Do what you are."[4]

What I appreciate about Jesus's admittedly sad synagogue snub is the way it highlights His unyielding commitment to His calling. Though many Bible scholars believe Jesus was aware of His divinity by the time He taught in the temple at the age of twelve, Scripture doesn't tell us exactly when Jesus discovered His true identity. But once He did, there was no turning back. Jesus didn't stutter, stammer, or dumb down His mission in order to make those around Him more comfortable. He didn't say, "God is kind of…sort of…maybe going to use Me to save the world." Instead, He swung for the fence.

THE FREEDOM HE PROCLAIMS
BY SWINGING AWAY

A very insistent woman recently interrupted a conversation I was having with someone else to announce that God had told her I needed to quit my job, move to another city, and change vocational direction or He wasn't going to bless me. I was a little flustered. First, I hadn't asked for her opinion; second, she didn't know me from Adam; and third, her "prophecy" wasn't in a healthy biblical context. After an awkward moment I politely said I'd consider her words, because God tends to speak in unusual ways. And since the Bible promises He gives clear directions,[5] I knew He'd either confirm or refute what she'd just said. Of course after praying about it, the Holy Spirit confirmed what my gut had already sensed: this chick was way off base!

If five years ago I'd been confronted by a stranger insisting she knew God's will for my life, I probably would have been more than momentarily flustered. I probably would've gobbled extra carbohydrates for days to sop up my anxiety and lost precious hours of sleep worrying about whether or not I was in the role I was created to fulfill. But, thankfully, I've been largely liberated from thinking that critics know what's best for me, and I have newfound security about the way I'm wired. I *know* I'm where God wants and doing what He's called me to, for the time being. Which means I won't be running out for boxes and packing up my house anytime soon!

The Old Testament passage Jesus intentionally selected (and translated from Hebrew to Aramaic) when He preached to His hometown crowd speaks directly to the kind of secure liberty we can enjoy because of Him:

The Spirit of the Lord GOD is upon me,
  because the LORD has anointed me
to bring good news to the poor;
  he has sent me to bind up the brokenhearted,
to proclaim liberty to the captives,
  and the opening of the prison to those who are
    bound;
to proclaim the year of the LORD's favor… *Isaiah 61:1–2*

The last line is key. "The year of the LORD's favor" refers to the year of jubilee when, according to Leviticus 25:8–12, Israel was commanded to celebrate *absolute* liberty. God told His people this restfest was to take place once every fifty years, and during that season they were to take a break from labor, to give the land a break from being plowed, and to give people in financial trouble the undeserved break of having all their debt cancelled. It was essentially a *super-Sabbath,* which meant they got a really long vacation, and the entire amount they'd accrued on their Target Visas was forgiven. The year of jubilee was an unprecedented explosion of emancipation!

Therefore, when Jesus swung for the fence by saying *He* was ushering in the year of the Lord's favor, He was promising liberty to everyone who believes in Him. Which means we can take a permanent vacation from trying to live up to other people's expectations, and we can rest assured that the debt of every single mistake we've made—or will make in the future—has been forgiven. We are therefore released to live and work and play as the redeemed and adored children of God!

So by all means, take a break and breathe in the sweet smell of freedom, then pick up the gifts your Creator has blessed you with and swing away for His glory!

We need an untamed *Savior because...* only a *wildly confident* Jesus can free us to trust in the liberty He brings and to live boldly as a result.

■ ■ Living and Loving with Abandon ■ ■

1. How would you describe the difference between confidence and arrogance?

2. Who's the most confident person in your sphere of relationships? Does that person's secure sense of self tend to make you more comfortable or less comfortable? Why?

3. Read Psalm 27. What specific lyrics in this song about having security in God—no matter how hard life gets—resonate the most with you?

4. Reread Luke 4:16. What's the underlying message of church attendance being Jesus's "custom"?

5. Read Isaiah 61:1–4. By this point in Jesus's ministry, how would you describe the way He'd literally fulfilled this prophecy about the year of the Lord's favor?

6. Using Eric Liddell's inspirational "When I run, I feel his pleasure" declaration as a template, how would you fill in the following: "When I _____, I feel God's pleasure"?

8

The Divine Trait of Stepping on Toes

Our Savior Is *Wildly* Confrontational

> Woe to the person who smoothly, flirtatiously, commandingly, convincingly preaches some soft, sweet something which is supposed to be Christianity.
>
> —SØREN KIERKEGAARD

recently spent more than a week in Texas in a program centered around an experience-based training plan originally created by Dr. Phil McGraw. Essentially, it serves as a rehab center for the heart. But it's not for the faint of heart. To begin with, I was assigned a complete stranger to bunk with in a hotel near a busy airport. Then I was ushered into a cave masquerading as a basement conference room. Several men and women wearing dark suits and grim faces were soberly introduced as the leaders for the program. Drill sergeants and funeral directors are positively giddy compared to this crew.

There we dove into eight days and nights of the most intense group "therapy" imaginable. (The staff insists the program is *not* therapy, but after ten years of Christian counseling, I think they're simply arguing semantics.) Everything in their agenda is geared toward breaking down defenses and building trust within the class. And the process worked like a charm. Insecurities quickly rose to the surface and tumbled from our trembling lips. Preconceived judgments came crawling out from the dark crevasses of our tired souls. The props of vocational success, composure, and good communication skills were aggressively kicked out from underneath all of us until we were willing to be completely truthful about whatever had been keeping us from consistently living the abundant and authentic life God created us to enjoy.

On the outside I probably didn't appear quite as desperate as some of the other men and women in our class (all of whom I grew to love with a depth that surprised me, given our lack of real-life experience together). I don't have nicotine stains on my fingers. I've never been to an AA meeting. I don't have any noticeable Tourette's-type tics. I generally look people in the eyes when having a conversation with them. Unless I'm in really bad traffic, expletives aren't part of my everyday vocabulary. And other than scars and cellulite, I don't have any colorful body art. No floral tattoos winding around my wrist or silver hoops piercing my eyebrows. I'm just an average-looking forty-six-year-old woman. Yet beneath my J.Jill exterior lies a heart crushed by childhood molestation that sometimes causes me to wonder whether I'm really worth another person's love and commitment.

The crucible of that eight-day healing journey, which took place in the unlikely Eden of a chain hotel, happened when the president of the program confronted me in front of everybody. He got right in my face and declared harshly into the microphone, "Lisa, you're a hypocrite. By not forgiving the people who abused you, you've put yourself above God. You're effectively saying your standard is higher than His. Do you have any idea how arrogant that is? How does it feel to talk to other people about the grace of the gospel yet not live what you're teaching?"

I could've argued I was only a little girl when my innocence was ripped away and it wasn't my responsibility to initiate forgiveness since my abusers had never even acknowledged or apologized for what they'd so cruelly taken. I could've defensively explained how I've done my very best to deal with the consequences of that trauma through Christian counseling and mentoring relationships. I could've whined and accused him of exaggerating the facts.

Instead, I replied, "It feels terrible." Because the essence of Kevin's accusation was true, and a corner of my heart has been stubbornly self-protective for as long as I can remember.

> What is the harshest truth spoken to you recently by someone who cares about you?

Kevin didn't eviscerate me to prove how intuitive he is. He wasn't trying to beat me down so I'd ultimately give in and sign up to participate in some multilevel marketing scheme to sell church ladies on Bible covers with hidden compartments for dark chocolate. Kevin expressed his observation because he cares about me. He knew I'd been stuck for a while and wanted me to forge ahead and experience the *complete* healing God makes available for broken hearts. He knocked me off balance with what some might call a below-the-belt jab, because he knew it would take brute force to slay the dragon of shame that'd been loitering in my soul for forty years. His unflinching honesty was motivated by kindness, and I will always be grateful for the role he played in helping untie the cords of unworthiness that had held my heart captive for far too long.

Our Savior is brutally honest as well. He often scorched the earth with verbal missiles to get sinners' attention. He did so because He longs for unbelievers to repent and be reconciled into the loving embrace of God and because He longs for Christians to grow in faith and maturity.

Jesus's compassion for lost, lonely, and mistake-prone people is the catalyst that drives Him to be *wildly confrontational.*

When Jesus Has Your Back, You Don't Have to Back Down

The Gospels reveal many instances when Jesus's candid remarks initially rattled the cage of propriety yet ultimately galvanized His followers. One such incident takes place in the middle of Matthew's gospel account:

> Do not think that I have come to bring peace to the earth. I have not come to bring peace, but a sword. For I have come to set a man against his father, and a daughter against her mother, and a daughter-in-law against her mother-in-law. And a person's enemies will be those of his own household. Whoever loves father or mother more than me is not worthy of me, and whoever loves son or daughter more than me is not worthy of me. *Matthew 10:34–37*

Yikes! This isn't the warm, fuzzy Jesus we're used to seeing on flannelgraph boards or stained-glass windows, is it? He's not wearing a lamb

The *Wild* Ways of God

Luke's gospel account records a similar hard saying of Jesus (Luke 12:49–53), except he replaces the saber metaphor with the theme of division. Luke's point is that Jesus is the "Great Divider" of humanity, because some people will repent and follow Him while others will reject the gospel and run headlong toward self-destruction and eternal separation from God.

around His neck and a pensive expression here. Instead, He sounds like someone who's managed to work Himself into a testosterone-fueled frenzy.

But the real meaning of Scripture isn't always what it initially seems to be, and we have to back up a bit before we can clearly understand the message of Jesus's saber metaphor.

First of all, the *analogy of Scripture* confirms that Jesus wasn't an angry, bloodthirsty warmonger who advocated conflict. In fact, earlier in Matthew during His Sermon on the Mount, He encouraged believers not to retaliate when they were mistreated, saying, "Blessed are the peacemakers, for they shall be called sons of God" (Matthew 5:9). And during His last visit to Jerusalem, Jesus wept over its lack of divine peace: "I wish you knew today what would bring you peace" (Luke 19:42, NCV). Finally, the message the disciples preached after Jesus's death and resurrection was commonly called the "gospel of peace" (Ephesians 6:15) or the "message of reconciliation" (2 Corinthians 5:19). Therefore we know that Jesus—*the Prince of Peace*—wasn't attempting to stir up turmoil or start a fight.

When Jesus spoke ominously about flashing blades and sparring families, He was not explaining the *purpose* of His ministry; He was describing the *effect.* Remember, Jesus had firsthand experience regarding the painful reality of a family divided over the gospel; His own brothers and sisters had rejected Him.[1] He knew many of His followers would suffer the same sorrow when their brother, sister, mother, father, spouse, or child rejected God's grace. So our Savior warned about the painful fallout that inevitably occurs within some families yet explained His expectation of absolute allegiance even when our faith causes a rift with our loved ones.

His words may sound harsh—certainly impolite—but there were probably empathetic tears in His eyes when He spoke them. Jesus loves and values His followers so much that He refuses to water down the truth for us. He won't shield us from the painful realities that accompany a life of faith, thereby causing us to grow up weak, wobbly, and easily defeated. Instead, He stands faithfully beside His beloved with one hand on our backs and the other holding a sword, which gives us the courage to open our eyes and look *hard and scary* right in the face.

■ ■ ■ ■ ■ ■ ■ ■ ■ Did You Know... ■ ■ ■ ■ ■ ■ ■ ■ ■

The term *analogy of Scripture* refers to using the entirety of God's Word to interpret a particular scripture; the scope and significance of one passage is better understood by relating it to others. The Westminster Confession explains this principle further: "The infallible rule of interpretation of Scripture is the Scripture itself: and therefore, when there is a question about the true and full sense of any Scripture (which is not manifold, but one), it must be searched and known by other places that speak more clearly."[2]

The courage Christ gives believers not to cave when our calling gets rough reminds me of a true story that took place almost seven hundred years ago. Caterina di Giacomo di Benincasa was born in Siena, Italy, in 1347, the twenty-fourth of twenty-five children in a poor but devout Catholic family. By the age of seven, she promised her virginity to God; at fifteen she cut off her hair so as to rebuff the romantic notions of neighborhood boys; and at eighteen she took vows to become a Dominican nun.[3] Saint Catherine of Siena, as she would later come to be called, spent the rest of her life helping the poor and nursing lepers. When stories about her vibrant faith, profound humility, and selfless acts of kindness reached Pope Gregory XI, he summoned her to a face-to-face meeting in Avignon, France.

In his book *Jesus Mean and Wild*, Mark Galli describes what happened next:

> When she met the Vicar of Christ, she blurted out that in the very place where all heavenly virtues should flourish, she only smelled the stink of hell's putrefaction.
>
> Catherine was referring to the glittering pomp of the Avignon papacy, where church offices were sold to the highest bidder and pope, cardinals, and bishops sported silk and jewels, and their houses were trimmed with gold and ivory. Meanwhile the threadbare clothing, crumbling shelters, and malnourished bodies of Christians across Europe went unnoticed by the papal bureaucrats. Catherine thought she would remind the pope, not so gently, of the contrast.
>
> The pope, a man not easily intimidated, wryly asked how Catherine, a recent visitor to Avignon, could possibly know about his odor: "How have you, who have been here such a short time, got such knowledge of all that goes on here?"
>
> Catherine didn't miss a beat. She replied that she had smelled the stench while she was still in Siena, some four hundred miles away. "I smelt the stink of the sins which flourish in the papal court while I was still at home."[4]

I'll bet the velvet-clad clergy surrounding Catherine of Siena and Pope Gregory gasped in disbelief! And I can't help but wonder if Cathy was shaking in her boots when she bravely told the truth. Yet she still chose to take a stand and voice observations that were jarring, some would even say harsh. Her wildly honest words surely rattled that stuffy fourteenth-century audience, but they didn't dishonor God. Instead, He was probably beaming with Fatherly pride when she didn't back down in the face of a blatant distortion of the gospel.

KRISPY KREMES AND FRUIT TREES

Before I traded in my Harley Davidson custom anniversary-edition Sportster for a green Italian scooter—earning scorn from the Harley community and immediately rebranding my image from cool biker chick to pizza-delivery person—I used to love taking my friend Kim's boys for motorcycle rides. However, Benjamin was so little when I got the bike that I only let him ride with me ever so slowly around their quiet neighborhood. And before I'd roll away from the curb, I'd lecture him on the importance of keeping both arms wrapped tightly around me at all times, even though we would be traveling at a top speed of ten miles an hour. Still, I'd have to stop in the middle of almost every joyride because Benji would loosen his grip to wave joyfully at passersby.

One afternoon I was giving him a second sermon about safety and had just sternly declared, "Benjamin, if you can't keep your arms tight around my tummy, I'm not going to take you on any more motorcycle rides!" In response he squeezed my middle with his little fingers and said with a grin, "You've been eating some Krispy Kremes, haven't you, Lisa?" Leave it to a seven-year-old to cut through the proverbial—and literal—

fat with an unfiltered indictment. And let me tell you, his innocent straight talk worked: not once since that day have I been tempted to turn into the Krispy Kreme parking lot, even when the "hot" sign was beckoning!

The next confrontational scene we're going to explore depicts Jesus issuing a much more sobering indictment on an entire people group. This particular altercation took place the day before and the day after Jesus booted a bunch of money-hungry schemers out of the temple, so there's actually a confrontation within a confrontation:

> As they left Bethany the next day, he was hungry. Off in the
> distance he saw a fig tree in full leaf. He came up to it expect-
> ing to find something for breakfast, but found nothing but fig
> leaves. (It wasn't yet the season for figs.) He addressed the tree:
> "No one is going to eat fruit from you again—ever!" And his
> disciples overheard him. *Mark 11:12–14, MSG*

Mark's narrative doesn't note what expressions the disciples were wearing after eavesdropping on their Savior scolding a tree, but I imagine they at least raised their eyebrows. Maybe they even wondered aloud if skipping breakfast had made Him lightheaded. I mean, who in their right mind actually addresses a tree? But evidently no one insisted on veering off course to look for a McDonald's; instead, the ragtag band kept trudging on toward the holy city.

> They arrived at Jerusalem. Immediately on entering the Tem-
> ple Jesus started throwing out everyone who had set up shop
> there, buying and selling. He kicked over the tables of the

bankers and the stalls of the pigeon merchants. He didn't let anyone even carry a basket through the Temple. And then he taught them, quoting this text:

> My house was designated a house of prayer for
> > the nations;
> You've turned it into a hangout for thieves.

> The high priests and religion scholars heard what was going on and plotted how they might get rid of him. They panicked, for the entire crowd was carried away by his teaching.
> At evening, Jesus and his disciples left the city. *Mark 11:15–19, MSG*

Yikes! Talk about confrontational. When Jesus and His disciples arrived at the temple and found the sanctity of His Father's house had been sullied by crass commercialism, He didn't hesitate to lambaste the perpetrators. Plus, the exorbitant prices the merchants were charging for animals to sacrifice made it impossible for the poor to participate in worship. This really aggravated Jesus, because He has a special place in His heart for the underprivileged.[5]

The confrontation escalated to a physical standoff when He literally blocked those trying to traipse through the courts with their baskets of wares. The fact that His fellow Jews were willing to violate the sacredness of the temple simply to have a convenient shortcut appalled Jesus. No wonder He turned on His heel and left Jerusalem in a huff.

In the morning, walking along the road, they saw the fig tree, shriveled to a dry stick. Peter, remembering what had happened the previous day, said to him, "Rabbi, look—the fig tree you cursed is shriveled up!" *Mark 11:20–21, MSG*

At the beginning of this passage, Jesus appears to be in a foul mood since He lambasted a fig tree for the minor infraction of not having fruit for Him to munch on, even though it wasn't in season. Which seems like one of those times when a parent unreasonably whacks the innocent kid because surely he'll deserve to be spanked for something in the future. Not only does Jesus come across as grouchy; He also seems less than green when He bashes a sapling.

Once again it's difficult to understand the entire application of Christ's message by simply skimming the black-and-white words of this passage. His point becomes much clearer when we consider this incident took place during the spring, when fig trees sport both foliage and a crop of small knobs the size of almonds (called *taqsh* in Palestinian Arabic) that serve as a forerunner to the real figs, which will appear about six weeks later.[6] So when Jesus found "nothing but fig leaves" (Mark 11:13, MSG), He knew this particular nubless perennial would never bear fruit and was therefore useless.

Furthermore, Jesus wasn't simply cursing unproductive vegetation; He was using the fruitless tree as a prophetic symbol for Israel's hypocrisy. God's chosen people had stopped producing the real fruit of relationship with Him through prayer and worship and were instead engaged in the showy but spiritually barren practice of ritual and legalism. By zapping a sterile tree, Jesus was making the emphatic point that our Creator will not allow unrepentant sinners to flourish indefinitely.

■ ■ ■ ■ ■ ■ ■ ■ **Did You Know...** ■ ■ ■ ■ ■ ■ ■ ■

The fig tree often symbolized Israel's relationship with
God in the Old Testament.[7] Fig trees were also used as a
symbol of peace and prosperity.[8] And a "poultice of figs"
was the prescription Isaiah used to cure King Hezekiah's
life-threatening infection (2 Kings 20:1–11, NIV).

THE RADIANT RESULTS OF RADICAL TRUTH

In much the same way that pressure applied to a lump of coal can produce diamonds, the hard-hitting truths of Jesus produce radiant results
in those who listen and believe. For instance, some of our Savior's
sharpest rebukes were aimed at the disciples, who went on to preach the
gospel around the ancient world and establish the New Testament
church:

> Peter said, "Explain the parable to us."
> "Are you still so dull?" Jesus asked them. *Matthew
> 15:15–16, NIV*

In other words, *Good night, guys, quit being such spiritual dingbats!*
And then there was the time Jesus singled out Pete with what seemed to
be a below-the-belt reprimand:

> From that time on Jesus began telling his followers that he
> must go to Jerusalem, where the Jewish elders, the leading
> priests, and the teachers of the law would make him suffer

many things. He told them he must be killed and then be raised from the dead on the third day.

Peter took Jesus aside and told him not to talk like that. He said, "God save you from those things, Lord! Those things will never happen to you!"

Then Jesus said to Peter, "Go away from me, Satan! You are not helping me! You don't care about the things of God, but only about the things people think are important."
Matthew 16:21–23, NCV

I can totally picture Pete grabbing Jesus by the elbow and steering Him out of earshot of the other disciples to exclaim, "Look, Jesus, I really wish you wouldn't talk like that. Surely nothing so horrible is going to happen to you!" Peter's resistance was obviously motivated by deep affection. But Jesus still lowered a devastating verbal boom and called Pete "Satan," a common Hebrew term meaning "adversary,"[9] so Jesus wasn't necessarily comparing him to the literal devil. He simply refused to let Peter go on blindly believing that nothing bad was going to happen. The Lamb who was headed toward slaughter forced His friend to face that fact.

If Jesus had let the disciples off the hook every time they were wrong—even when they were *sincerely* wrong—I doubt those guys would've matured into the men they became: crusading evangelists who bravely endured persecution, all but one ultimately dying a martyr's death for the cause of Christ.

In Marilyn McEntyre's *Christianity Today* article "Furthermore: Nice Is Not the Point," she wrote, "One of my husband's finer moments in parenting came one day when, after he had uttered an unwelcome word of correction to a disgruntled child, he leaned down, looked her in the eye, and said, 'Honey, this is what love looks like.' "[10]

So too, love didn't always look—or sound—nice when it passed through our Savior's lips. His words often left a welt on the hearts of those who were listening. He did not pull any punches. He did not subscribe to a religion of polite white lies. Yet every single thing our Messiah said was motivated by mercy. Jesus confronted confusion, oppression, dishonesty, and spiritual deadness because He cares so much about us and isn't willing to let us settle for anything less than the abundant life and absolute freedom God created for us to enjoy.

We need an untamed *Savior because...*
only a *wildly confrontational* Jesus can free us from faking our way through faith or accepting a counterfeit gospel so that He can mature us into brave, true believers.

■ ■ Living and Loving with Abandon ■ ■

1. Women of Faith *Connection* magazine writer Lisa Whittle describes real friends via the "Haircut Theory" explaining, "The surefire way to find out who your real friends are is to get a bad haircut and see who tells you it looks great. If she does and it's really as jacked up as you think, she is not a true girlfriend. A real friend will not lie to you just so you will keep getting that jacked-up haircut and thereby, won't look cuter than her."[11] In light of the Haircut Theory on friendship, how many real friends do you estimate having? Who do you think would list you as one of her real friends?

2. Read Proverbs 27:6. How would you summarize this worthy saying in modern-day language?

3. Describe a time when the stark reality of God's truth pointed out sin previously unnoticed—or at least unconfessed!—in your own life. What verse or passage of Scripture confirmed the error of your ways, and how did the Holy Spirit bring it to your attention (for example, in a Bible study, in a devotional time, in a greeting card, on a refrigerator magnet)?

4. Read the spoken parable of the barren fig tree in Luke 13:6–9. How does it compare to the "parable in action" we find in Mark 11:12–21?

5. How does Mark's "sandwich" technique of using one story to frame another in Mark 11:12–21 help us better understand Jesus's message about God's pending judgment? How does a pretentious

yet barren fig tree relate to the bustling religious business that was taking place in the temple?

6. Read Matthew 18:15–17 and Galatians 6:1. With regard to truth telling, how would you describe the significance between being right and being righteous?

9

Refreshingly Radical

Our Savior Is *Wildly* Unconventional

In terms of the world's sanity, Jesus is crazy as a coot, and anybody who thinks he can follow him without being a little crazy too is laboring less under a cross than under a delusion.

—FREDERICK BUECHNER

■ ■ ■ ■ ■ ■

This past Saturday I decided to celebrate my rare weekend at home by puttering around in the garden. However, before I had the chance to linger over new rosebuds or smell the blooming purple lavender, I was distracted by Harley's and Dottie's shrill, incessant barking. When I rounded the corner to see what they were making such a fuss about, I was horrified by the sight of a massive mottled black and tan snake, coiled and striking at them.

I really, really hate snakes. I think they epitomize all that is gross and scary on our planet. Coupled with slow drivers in the fast lane and smarmy men wearing pinkie rings and excessive cologne, they are the bane of my existence. Normally when I see one, I race wide-eyed with fear in the opposite direction. But this huge, hateful viper was threatening my dogs, so I swallowed my panic and started heaving landscaping rocks at it. Which prompted it to turn its beady eyes my way and begin striking *at me*!

I don't know if you've ever had a five-foot serpent doing its best to bite you, but it'll definitely press your survival button. Silently responding, *I don't think so, big boy*, I ran to the garage to get a pellet gun, then proceeded to fire away. Of course my hands were shaking so badly it's a wonder I didn't shoot my own foot or a neighbor! Luckily part of the pellet barrage hit the mark, and Mr. Wiggly ultimately gave up the ghost.

That creepy-crawler episode lasted only a few minutes (it took much longer for my pulse to return to normal), but I've thought about it all weekend. I can still picture its undulating, serpentine body and the way its mouth gaped open when it lunged forward to strike. It could have been the star of a late-night horror movie. And I feel absolutely no remorse about riddling that sucker with holes!

> What's the scariest or most repulsive creature you've ever had to go toe-to-toe with? What was the outcome of your confrontation?

In light of my extreme aversion to slithery things, I find it interesting that Jesus compared the Pharisees—the very guys whose approval would've been politically beneficial for Him—to snakes. He didn't play nice with the powerful God Squad; He publicly denounced them. And while He could've tempered His comments and compared them to more innocuous creatures such as three-toed sloths, possums, or armadillos, He went for the jugular of animal metaphors and described them instead as a brood of vipers!

His disparaging remarks infuriated those influential leaders and proved our Redeemer to be *wildly unconventional.*

YOU CAN'T JUDGE A RELIGIOUS BOOK BY ITS COVER

I haven't always been scared of snakes. In fact, when I was a kid, I thought the little ones were kind of cute—until one Saturday afternoon when I was eleven or twelve. My stepbrother, Ricky, was engrossed in a solitary game of Pong (one of the original home video games, which I think could supplant waterboarding as an effective torture device) and kept rebuffing my pleas to play outside. So I traipsed down to the barn, thinking I would saddle my horse, Gypsy, and explore the fields and orange groves that flanked our property. But I got distracted when I saw something moving inside a white bucket near the tack room. I peered inside and was delighted to find a wee snake that looked very lonely.

Being an adventuresome tomboy, I reached in and picked it up by the tail. It wriggled and arched and tried to bite me, which I thought was funny because it was only about a foot long and obviously just a harmless baby. I don't remember how long I'd been playing with it—maybe five or ten minutes—when my dad walked into the barn. He stopped dead in his tracks and held up his hands—as if he were surrendering at gunpoint—and said gently but firmly, "Lisa, I want you to put that snake back in the bucket very slowly."

I could tell by the tone of his voice he meant business, so I carefully plopped my new friend back into its plastic habitat. That's when Dad told me I'd been fooling around with a pygmy rattlesnake, which though petite is an extremely poisonous member of the pit viper family. They're also reputed to be hot-tempered rascals that strike repeatedly at the slightest provocation.[1]

At first glance the Pharisees didn't look poisonous either. They were prominent members of Jewish society, respected by the regular Joes, because they were educated, while the *Am-ha-Aretz*, or "people of the land," were illiterate. And the Pharisees weren't just a bunch of eggheads loitering around in coffee shops philosophizing, either. They were industrious, spending long hours in synagogues hunched over copies of the Torah (the first five books of the Old Testament, also known as the

*Penta*teuch, since *penta* means five) so as to interpret the words God narrated to Moses into a comprehensive list of behavioral guidelines. Much like the Taliban enforces Islamic fundamentalist rules in parts of Afghanistan and Pakistan, the Pharisees enforced what they thought were Jehovah's rules in ancient Israel. They were, in effect, the moral police.

Unfortunately, they were more concerned about *looking* spiritual than about *loving* the people around them. Which is evidenced by the oh-so-picky parameters they created and enforced. They were meticulous about the details of ritual purity—like whether or not you could have cheese on your hamburger, what exact length to wear your hair, what shade of blue the tassels on prayer shawls had to be, how to decorate phylacteries, and how to cover skin imperfections like warts. They were also obsessive about tithing, probably because when synagogue funds dried up, so did their paychecks. But their passion for religious minutiae robbed them of compassion for their fellowman. They began separating themselves from people who weren't as fastidious, assuming any inter-personal association would jeopardize their purity. In fact, the Greek word translated as "Pharisee" in the New Testament is *Pharisaios,* which means "separate ones."[2]

■ ■ ■ ■ ■ ■ ■ ■ ■ **Did You Know...** ■ ■ ■ ■ ■ ■ ■ ■

Phylacteries are small leather boxes that observant Jews wear on their upper left arm and forehead in adherence to Exodus 13:9, 16 and Deuteronomy 6:8. The boxes contain small scrolls with passages from both Exodus and Deuteronomy.

And when they enforced their soul-crushing belief system on the Am-ha-Aretz, convincing them that they would never be good enough for God, Jesus called those scaly scholars on the carpet:

Then Jesus said to the crowds and to his disciples: "The teachers of the law and the Pharisees sit in Moses' seat. So you must obey them and do everything they tell you. But do not do what they do, for they do not practice what they preach. They tie up heavy loads and put them on men's shoulders, but they themselves are not willing to lift a finger to move them.

"Everything they do is done for men to see: They make their phylacteries wide and the tassels on their garments long; they love the place of honor at banquets and the most important seats in the synagogues; they love to be greeted in the marketplaces and to have men call them 'Rabbi.'

"But you are not to be called 'Rabbi,' for you have only one Master and you are all brothers. And do not call anyone on earth 'father,' for you have one Father, and he is in heaven. Nor are you to be called 'teacher,' for you have one Teacher, the Christ. The greatest among you will be your servant. For whoever exalts himself will be humbled, and whoever humbles himself will be exalted.

"Woe to you, teachers of the law and Pharisees, you hypocrites! You shut the kingdom of heaven in men's faces. You yourselves do not enter, nor will you let those enter who are trying to. . . .

"You snakes! You brood of vipers! How will you escape being condemned to hell?" *Matthew 23:1–13, 33, NIV*

If you want to get our Redeemer all riled up, just start looking down your nose at people around you and preach the message that only a select few—including yourself, of course—have earned the right to be in relationship with God. Our Messiah gets *really* ticked off when arrogant posers try to prevent those outside their clique from experiencing His mercy and compassion!

It would've been politically expedient for Jesus to align Himself with the Pharisees. They were well connected. They controlled the programming for the religious radio and television networks. They could've made Him a star. But Jesus wasn't motivated by power, celebrity, or popularity, and He couldn't be bought, coerced, or bullied. Nothing was more important to Jesus than accomplishing the task His Father had given Him: to rescue the lost. Therefore Jesus bucked wildly against the saddle of discrimination.

■ ■ ■ ■ ■ ■ ■ The *Wild* Ways of God ■ ■ ■ ■ ■ ■ ■

The word *hypocrite* isn't found anywhere else in Scripture except Matthew, Mark, and Luke and is spoken only by Jesus. This Greek term actually means "stage actor"[3] and would have been highly offensive to the Pharisees in light of their staunch opposition to Greco-Roman entertainment. They were especially mortified by what went on in the theater, because many ancient plays featured full nudity and pornographic material, so for Jesus to call them actors was as bad as calling them snakes. It was a wild zinger of an accusation!

DARK LIPSTICK ISN'T A DISQUALIFIER

Although the official sect of Pharisees flourished in Jewish culture during the first century, plenty of people who unofficially subscribe to their mind-set are lurking around in modern Christian culture. As a matter of fact, I ran into one recently. She was well dressed and armed with a big Bible and a sweet Southern accent. She approached me at the end of a retreat where I'd been the guest speaker and drawled, "I was very surprised to see you walk up to the podium on Friday night because when I noticed you at registration, I thought you were one of those *non-Christians* we were supposed to invite this weekend."

Suppressing a grin, I asked, "What was it about me that made you assume I *wasn't* a Christian?"

She paused for a long moment, then leaned toward me and confided in a disdainful whisper, "Well, you were wearing those chunky shoes and that dark lipstick."

I've searched the Scriptures and can't find anywhere that Jesus mandates stodgy footwear and sheer lipstick for believers. Yet that legalistic lady was convinced I was a pagan, disqualified to be a follower of Jesus because of my Cole Haans and M•A•C Fresh Moroccan Frost!

I'm so glad our Savior doesn't demand that Christians look, think, or talk exactly alike. Because if I had to try to gain entry into some exclusive club of capable women who bake casseroles, are avid scrapbookers, and carry purses that perfectly match their shoes, I wouldn't make the cut! Instead, throughout the Gospels—from Jesus's unusual choice of teammates to His refusal to join the ruling gang of religious hotshots—our Savior advocated *unity,* not *uniformity.* In fact, during His earthly ministry Jesus was a magnet for those who were marginalized:

He was teaching in one of the meeting places on the Sabbath. There was a woman present, so twisted and bent over with arthritis that she couldn't even look up. She had been afflicted with this for eighteen years. When Jesus saw her, he called her over. "Woman, you're free!" He laid hands on her and suddenly she was standing straight and tall, giving glory to God. *Luke 13:10–13,* MSG

I can only imagine the sideways glances that followed this crooked woman wherever she went. In a culture where physical deformity was typically associated with warped morals, her neighbors surely assumed she was a reprobate and went out of their way to avoid her. (Remember in John 9:1–3 when the disciples, after meeting a man who'd been born blind, asked Jesus who had sinned: the man or his parents?) Yet instead of following the community consensus and shunning her, Jesus beckoned the bent lady. Then He placed His holy hands on her misshapen spine, and she was finally able to stand tall—literally and figuratively—for the first time in almost twenty years!

Then there was the case of the vertically challenged accountant:

Then Jesus entered and walked through Jericho. There was a man there, his name Zacchaeus, the head tax man and quite rich. He wanted desperately to see Jesus, but the crowd was in his way—he was a short man and couldn't see over the crowd. So he ran on ahead and climbed up in a sycamore tree so he could see Jesus when he came by.

When Jesus got to the tree, he looked up and said, "Zacchaeus, hurry down. Today is my day to be a guest in your home." Zacchaeus scrambled out of the tree, hardly believing his good luck, delighted to take Jesus home with him. Everyone who saw the incident was indignant and grumped, "What business does he have getting cozy with this crook?" *Luke 19:1–7, MSG*

Not only did this diminutive guy have to wear lifts in his shoes; he also had a reputation for financial fraud! Anyone who has endured the gauntlet of middle-school mockery can empathize with the pain of the derisive comments he surely endured: "Hey, Zach, did the ledger come up a little *short* today?" Yet Luke makes it clear that the kindness of Christ prompted big repentance in the little man:

Zacchaeus just stood there, a little stunned. He stammered apologetically, "Master, I give away half my income to the poor—and if I'm caught cheating, I pay four times the damages."

Jesus said, "Today is salvation day in this home! Here

■ ■ ■ ■ ■ ■ The *Wild* Ways of God ■ ■ ■ ■ ■ ■

Jesus's ministry was so unconventional. He didn't have a physical address. He didn't enjoy the convenience of a downtown office or even a spare room with a file cabinet in some synagogue basement. Instead, He and the disciples spent the better part of three years *camping*.[4] The King of kings loves us so much that He left the courts of heaven and went without clean sheets or running water to bring us living hope!

he is: Zacchaeus, son of Abraham! For the Son of Man came to find and restore the lost." *Luke 19:8–10,* MSG

Jesus didn't swim with the social tide and ostracize the wee embezzler with whom He presumably had nothing in common. Instead, He took the time to visit his home and share a meal. It's amazing how grace can bridge every philosophical, psychological, socioeconomic, and demographic gap.

WHO'S SITTING IN YOUR SOCIAL CIRCLE?

I'm not a big fan of chain letters, multilevel marketing opportunities, or those cheesy morality tales that are forwarded in bulk on the Internet. However, someone e-mailed me a story last year that was so compelling I couldn't stop thinking about it while writing this chapter about how wildly unconventional Jesus is. It goes something like this:

His name is Bill. He has wild hair, wears a T-shirt with holes in it, jeans, and no shoes. This was literally his wardrobe for his entire four years of college. He is brilliant. He is kind of profound and very, very bright. He became a Christian while attending college.

Across the street from the campus is a well-dressed, very conservative church. They want to develop a ministry to the students but are not sure how to go about it.

One day Bill decides to go there. He walks in with no shoes, jeans, his T-shirt full of holes, and wild hair. The service has already started, so Bill starts down the aisle, looking for a seat.

The church is completely packed, and he can't find a seat. By now, people are really looking a bit uncomfortable, but no one says anything. Bill gets closer and closer and closer to the pulpit, and when he realizes there are no seats, he just sits down right on the carpet. By now the people are really uptight, and the tension in the air is thick.

About this time the minister realizes that from way at the back of the church, a deacon is slowly making his way toward Bill. Now the deacon, in his eighties, has silver gray hair and wears a three-piece suit. He is a godly man and very elegant, very dignified, very courtly. He walks with a cane, and as he starts walking toward this boy, everyone is saying to themselves that you can't blame him for what he's going to do. How can you expect a man of his age and his background to understand some college kid on the floor?

It takes a long time for the man to reach the boy. The church is utterly silent except for the clicking of the man's cane. All eyes are focused on him. You can't even hear anyone breathing. The minister can't even preach the sermon until the deacon does what he has to do.

And then, to their amazement, they see this elderly man drop his cane on the floor and lower himself to sit down next to Bill. There he worships with the young man so he won't be alone.

Everyone chokes up with emotion. When the minister gains control, he says: "What I'm about to preach, you will never remember. What you have just seen, you will never forget."[5]

I've spent hours online trying to find out when and where this event took place. Did it occur in the East or in the West? In a big city or a small town? Was Bill in his early twenties or an older grad student? But I haven't been able to dig up any more details than those printed here. Frankly, I couldn't even verify this event actually happened. But if it didn't, it *should have.* How awesome would it be if courtly deacons were rubbing shoulders with crazy-haired college kids in our churches? If women in crop pants, on their way home from Bible study, could be found at gas stations chatting up bikers in black leather?

■ ■ ■ The *Wild* Ways of God's People ■ ■ ■

Following Jesus often prompts Christians to make unconventional life choices too. Like Pastor Francis Chan, who returned to California following a mission trip in Africa and proceeded to sell his home and move into one half that size in order to have more money to give away.

Or Nathan Barlow, a missionary to Ethiopia who had to be flown out of the country to receive medical attention for a terrible tooth infection. He was so determined not to leave the mission field again that he had a dentist pull out all his teeth and give him dentures so he could continue sharing the gospel uninterrupted.

Or the late Rich Mullins, an award-winning musician, who gave his earnings to his church, showed up at concerts barefoot, and sometimes confessed his shortcomings publicly so fans wouldn't put him on a pedestal.[6]

Jesus came into the world to redeem *sinners,* to restore lost and lonely people from every tribe and tongue into a loving relationship with our Creator God. Therefore He didn't limit His interaction to one socially acceptable slice of humanity. He hung out with white- and blue-collar folks. With conservatives and liberals. With benefactors and beggars. With criminals and attorneys. In fact, our Savior was accused of being a glutton and a drunk in light of some of the colorful company He kept![7]

As His ambassadors, may we seek to be every bit as inclusive with our affections.

We need an untamed *Savior because...* only a *wildly unconventional* Jesus can free us to abandon stereotypes and prejudice and truly love the world around us!

▪ ▪ Living and Loving with Abandon ▪ ▪

1. What are some examples of things you wear, say, or do—or that you avoid wearing, saying, or doing—mostly just to make others think you're a "good" Christian?

2. How would you describe a vibrant, authentic Christian? What aspects of your definition veer from the more conventional religious view that puts a premium on outward appearances? What part of your definition of being in a close relationship with Jesus could stand to be stretched in light of His disdain for hypocrisy?

3. Read Luke 6:27–36 and John 13:34–35. What parameters do these passages give regarding whom Christians are called to love?

4. Read Matthew 9:10–12. If you were paraphrasing verse 12, what word would you use in place of "sick"?

5. Read Acts 10:34–35. What are a few practical things Christians can do to be more impartial and thus more like our heavenly Father?

6. Read Revelation 7:9–10. What's the closest thing you've experienced to the kind of pan-national, multiethnic unity John describes in his vision of heaven?

10

Our Empathetic Hero

Our Savior Is *Wildly* Attentive

Compassion is the priesthood of Jesus.

—HENRI NOUWEN

■ ■ ■ ■ ■ ■

Have you ever heard comedian Jeff Foxworthy's hilarious "You Know You're a Redneck" routine? Well, I had my own "I'm a redneck" epiphany many years ago during my formative teen years. Our family was planning a road trip to take in the beauty of fall foliage and to visit my sister, who was attending college in North Carolina at the time. My stepfather, John, decided to drive his truck instead of our sedan so he could tote his entire collection of fishing paraphernalia to Asheville. Only three people could fit up front, and because my younger brother, John Price, was hyperactive and prone to jump out of vehicles moving at slow speeds, my parents decided I was the obvious candidate to ride in the back of the truck throughout the tristate journey.

You might notice a trace of residual bitterness due to the still-painful memory of having to fend for myself on a cot surrounded by coolers and camping supplies for 1,148 miles while the three of them listened to the radio and sipped Slurpees in the comfort of an air-conditioned cab. Did I mention I was a senior in high school when this excursion took place? I was seventeen and naturally concerned about my outward

157

appearance when we took that Griswold family vacation. At first I attempted to make the best of my open-air situation, thinking I could at least get a tan while traveling. But as soon as John started hurtling down the highway, I realized the fatal flaw in my strategy. I hadn't planned on the flying debris and sand in my face; it was like some sort of white-trash dermabrasion!

Within minutes I surrendered to a facedown position on the cot with my arms tucked under me while reciting the mantra, "My family is bonkers, my family is bonkers!" over and over again in my head. Of course it didn't take more than an hour of high-speed, wind-tunnel torture for me to be pockmarked, tangled, and grouchy. Then, to make matters much worse, something sharp and pointy got stuck in my eye. I tried to wipe out what I assumed was a giant shard of glass—probably tossed out the window by my gleeful sibling—but couldn't. It hurt like crazy, and I could feel wet streams rolling down my face. Which, of course, I assumed was blood. I comforted myself with the thought, *They're going to feel terrible when they find out I'm now blind in one eye!*

Finally I began banging on the back window of the cab, yelling, "Stop the truck! I'm bleeding!" However, I forgot there was a double-pane window between them and me, so my cries for help were completely ignored until the unholy trinity finally pulled over for a pit stop.

> When recently have you felt like, no matter how loud you screamed, your pleas for aid were falling on deaf ears?

I may've exaggerated just a bit in my recollection of that fateful expedition (and should also note that Mom put a stop to my being carted around in the back of the truck for long distances as soon as she found out it was illegal), but hopefully you still got the point about feeling unnoticed!

The remarkable truth about Jesus is, He will never ignore our pleas. He will not sit impassively while we signal desperately for help. In fact, we don't even have to signal; our Savior knows exactly what we need even when we don't express it. Peter said it best: "Give all your worries to him, because he cares about you" (1 Peter 5:7, NCV).

In other words, our Savior is *wildly attentive* to our needs!

GUT REACTIONS

One of my favorite Greek words is *splanchnon*. While it might sound like a yummy Middle Eastern pastry, it's actually a word my mother wouldn't let me use at the dinner table if she knew what it meant. Because the English translation is the "inward parts of the body" or "intestines"!

Lest you think I have a low-class vocabulary, let me explain why I like such a seemingly vulgar term. The word *splanchnon* is the root word for *splanchnizomai,* which is translated "filled with compassion" or "moved with pity" in the New Testament.[1] And it's the same word used to describe our Savior's reaction to many of the lame, blind, grieving, and diseased people He came into contact with. Which means Jesus wasn't emotionally distant from broken men, women, and children; the healing miracles He performed were prompted by deeply felt *gut* reactions.

For instance, there's a wonderful story near the beginning of Mark's gospel where the sensitivity of Jesus is exemplified:

> And a leper came to him, imploring him, and kneeling said
> to him, "If you will, you can make me clean." Moved with
> pity, he stretched out his hand and touched him and said to

him, "I will; be clean." And immediately the leprosy left him, and he was made clean. *Mark 1:40–42*

In his book *Where Is God When It Hurts?* Philip Yancey reports that leprosy is the oldest recorded disease and one of the most feared.[2] Author Ken Gire goes a step further and describes it in lurid detail:

> It's a horrible disease, leprosy. It begins with little specks on the eyelids and on the palms of the hand. Then it spreads over the body. It bleaches the hair white. It casts a cadaverous pallor over the skin, crusting it with scales and erupting over it with oozing sores.
>
> But that's just what happens on the surface. Penetrating the skin the disease, like a moth, eats its way through the network of nerves woven throughout the body's tissues. Soon the body becomes numb to the point of sensory deprivation, numbed to both pleasure and pain. A toe can break, and it will register no pain. And sensing no pain, the leper will continue walking, only to worsen the break and hasten the infection. One by one the appendages of the leper suffer their fate against the hard edges of life.[3]

Not only was leprosy a potentially crippling disease during the time of Christ, but it also poisoned its carriers with a crippling social stigma. In fact, according to Levitical law, lepers had to walk around in ripped clothes and unkempt hair yelling, "Unclean, unclean" whenever they were in public places so no one would approach them and become contaminated.[4] They were also commanded to live alone. Which means this poor guy in Mark 1 was an utter pariah. He'd likely lost contact with his family, had no friends outside the leper colony, and hadn't experienced the touch of another person in years. No backrubs after lugging furniture upstairs, no hugs on his birthday, no gentle hand wiping his tears away when he broke down and cried.

In light of the leper's hideous deformities and the distance a law-abiding Jew was expected to maintain from such a person, it would make sense for our Redeemer just to wave His hand, say something dramatic like "Shazam!" and heal the guy without any physical contact. Instead, our tender-hearted Savior reached out and touched the man *before* healing his gnarled body. The Son of God's gesture said, "I love you just the way you are. You matter to me." Moved with deep compassion, Christ healed the man's emotional wounds as well as his leprosy.

■ ■ ■ ■ ■ ■ ■ The *Wild* Ways of God ■ ■ ■ ■ ■ ■ ■

Matthew, Mark, Luke, and John record Jesus healing a combined total of thirty-five people. Yet probably thousands more healings weren't recorded, plus sometimes Jesus healed an entire—albeit not individually named—community.[5]

MENDING A MOTHER'S BROKEN HEART

Another *splanchnizoma* moment took place outside a cozy community called Nain:

> Soon afterwards Jesus went to a town called Nain, and his followers and a large crowd traveled with him. When he came near

the town gate, he saw a funeral. A mother, who was a widow, had lost her only son. A large crowd from the town was with the mother while her son was being carried out. *Luke 7:11–12, NCV*

This mama has a double whammy because she's lost her husband and her only son. Which means she's not just brokenhearted; she's about to be broke. She faces an uncertain future that may well include begging for her meals. Of course, she's not worrying about that or the pending mortgage payment right now. Instead, she's weeping with uncontrollable grief as she trudges alongside the pallbearers carrying her boy out of town in an open casket. She doesn't notice the gentle stranger who stops to stare at their sad parade.

That's why what happens next is so incredible. The wailing widow doesn't ask for a miracle—Luke's narrative implies she doesn't even know who Jesus is—yet the Lord of the universe compassionately crashes the funeral procession and grants one anyway:

When the Lord saw her, he felt very sorry for her and said, "Don't cry." He went up and touched the coffin, and the people who were carrying it stopped. Jesus said, "Young man, I tell you, get up!" And the son sat up and began to talk. Then Jesus gave him back to his mother. *Luke 7:13–15, NCV*

Can you imagine this mama's expression? I bet her eyes were as big as saucers and her hand flew up to cover her open mouth. She probably didn't let go of her son until he finally squeaked, "Mom, I can't breathe!" in gentle protest. And I'm pretty sure she didn't make him do any chores for at least a year or two!

Luke doesn't share the specifics of how she responded to the Messiah's unsolicited mercy, but he does describe the enthusiasm of the crowd who witnessed the kid's resurrection:

All the people were amazed and began praising God, saying, "A great prophet has come to us! God has come to help his people."

This news about Jesus spread through all Judea and into all the places around there. *Luke 7:16–17, NCV*

■ ■ ■ ■ ■ ■ ■ The *Wild* Ways of God ■ ■ ■ ■ ■ ■ ■

The healings Jesus performed were problematic for the scribes and Pharisees on several levels. First of all, the wow factor of Christological miracles incited crowds and diverted attention away from their brand of legalistic religiosity. Second, Jesus often pronounced a person's sins as forgiven when He healed the person,[6] which they believed was blasphemous since only Jehovah had the power to forgive sin.

OMNIPOTENT OPHTHALMOLOGIST

The last *splanchnizoma* story we're going to peruse takes place in the gospel written by Matt (the IRS agent turned preacher) and involves two boisterous men:

As they were leaving Jericho, a huge crowd followed. Suddenly they came upon two blind men sitting alongside the road. When they heard it was Jesus passing, they cried out, "Master, have mercy on us! Mercy, Son of David!" The crowd tried to hush them up, but they got all the louder, crying, "Master, have mercy on us! Mercy, Son of David!" *Matthew 20:29–31, MSG*

Unlike the widow who didn't even notice Immanuel, these guys were screaming their heads off trying to get His attention. It didn't matter that everyone was trying to shush them; the admonitions to "Be quiet!" only served to increase their rambunctious cries. It's as if they knew Jesus was their only hope, and they weren't about to let Him leave town without at least trying to heal them.

I wish there'd been a scrapbooker in the crowd that day because I'd love to know if my imagination is correct and Jesus was stifling a grin over their rowdiness! I think He was also pleased, in spite of their disorderly conduct, because they kept calling Him the "Son of David," indicating their faith in Him as the Messiah.

Jesus stopped and called over, "What do you want from me?" They said, "Master, we want our eyes opened. We want to see!" *Matthew 20:32–33, MSG*

In other words, "We want to see our children smile. We want to watch our wives brush their hair before bed. We want to read the Torah. We want to be able to see!"

And once more the Master of the universe is moved. His holy heart is engaged. Although Jesus knew the Cross was looming and He'd soon lose the companionship of His closest friends—and, much more significantly, the favor of His heavenly Father when He took the sin of the world on His shoulders—He still felt deep compassion and restored their vision:

> Deeply moved, Jesus touched their eyes. They had their sight
> back that very instant, and joined the procession. *Matthew*
> *20:34, MSG*

Jesus knew that—along with everyone else—they'd turn their backs on Him when the going got rough in Jerusalem. Yet when they began dancing a happy jig while traipsing along behind Him, He probably laughed out loud with pure joy over the return on His investment.

■ ■ ■ ■ ■ ■ ■ The *Wild* Ways of God ■ ■ ■ ■ ■ ■

Jesus sometimes associated a person's faith in Him with that person's healing.[7] But He also performed healing miracles for people who expressed no faith in Him whatsoever.[8]

REPUTABLE ISN'T A REQUIREMENT

One of the true gifts of having friends with families is borrowing their children. Whenever I feel the need to roast s'mores over the fire or go to an animated movie or get a sugary drink at Sonic, I can usually find someone who's more than willing to loan me her offspring for a few hours. But I've also received the unexpected gift of friendship with some of the husbands. Wendell Harris sweetly worries about my having to lift heavy stuff. Tom Flaherty talks with me on the phone when I call Judy and even invited me to join his search for the country's best barbeque. And Andrew Self not only teases me about my funky taste in shoes; he's the most honorable man I know. It didn't surprise me at all when he got elected as a trial court judge for the state of Kentucky after eighteen years of private law practice.

Perhaps because I've seen one too many movies and read one too many articles about corruption in America's judicial system, I'd developed a slightly pessimistic view of the bench. That is, until Judge Self picked up a gavel. I absolutely love the way he runs his courtroom. He treats every single person in his jurisdiction—even if someone's on trial for murder or drug trafficking—with respect. Although many of the men and women shuffle into his courtroom wearing orange jumpsuits and shackles, Andrew still greets them with a sincere "Good morning" or "Good afternoon" and always addresses them as "Mr." or "Miss" or "Mrs." He believes that treating felony suspects with common courtesy allows them to retain some measure of hope. Plus, he says, if we treat criminals with dignity to the extent we can, then when they get out of prison and return to society, they're more likely to behave like dignified citizens.

When "Buddy" shuffled into his courtroom one day, Andrew actually recognized him. Buddy was employed by a couple Andrew and Eva are friends with, so he and Andrew had spent an afternoon helping that couple move from one house to another. Andrew said it was surreal to be wearing a black robe and be on the bench above Buddy in light of the fact that "he'd carried one end of a dining table, and I'd carried the other." Plus, Buddy was a pitiable defendant. Years before, he'd been unfairly incarcerated (another judge mistakenly thought he'd violated parole), and while he was awaiting release, a mean con threw a container of boiling oil at him. He suffered extensive third-degree burns, resulting in horrible disfigurement.

Nonetheless, during the trial Andrew presided over, it was proven beyond a reasonable doubt that Buddy had committed a violent crime. And because he was a repeat offender, Andrew was compelled to impose a harsh sentence of seventeen years in the state penitentiary.

But before Buddy was led away, Andrew said he wanted to let Buddy know he believed that there was more to him, that he was capable of a life other than one of crime. So he looked directly into Buddy's eyes and paraphrased one of his favorite authors, Russian novelist Aleksandr Solzhenitsyn (a Christian who was persecuted by the Soviet KGB): "The line separating good and evil passes…right through every human heart."[9] Andrew held his gaze and, without any more words, conveyed the possibility of redemption…of a better life in which he could choose good instead of evil.

My friend doesn't hand out verdicts dispassionately from an ivory tower; his heart is moved by the accused men and women who stand before him. Their culpability doesn't negate his compassion. And so it is with our divine Judge.

If you're anything like me, you've wrestled with the connection between benevolence and merit. Perhaps you feel sympathy toward the victims of natural disasters yet have no pity for friends who are drowning in credit-card debt. You find it easier to pray for people suffering from cancer than for lifelong smokers struggling with emphysema. Maybe your heart is moved by orphans but hardened toward pro-choice picketers. What makes Jesus's investment of kindness so amazing is that He doesn't hedge His bets. He doesn't slosh healing mercy on the more reputable folks and just sprinkle it on the foolhardy.

Our Savior's love isn't limited by our relative deservedness. He is deeply concerned for every kind of sinner!

> *We need an* untamed *Savior because...*
> only a *wildly attentive* Jesus can meet our needs and free us from all sorts of physical, emotional, and social ailments.

■ ■ Living and Loving with Abandon ■ ■

1. If you could literally see incarnate Jesus walking by right now, would you shout to get His attention, walk over and tap Him on the shoulder, or just hope He noticed you? Explain your answer.

2. What's your favorite way to be shown attention by someone else (for example, physical touch, words of comfort, etc.)? What's the most common way for you to demonstrate your attentiveness to the needs and moods of others?

3. Read Matthew 6:25–34. How would your day tomorrow be different if you lived it as though you really believed Christ's promise in this passage?

4. Read Hebrews 2:10–18. Why do you think it's important for Jesus to be an empathetic hero?

5. Read 2 Corinthians 1:3–4. How have your own needs enabled you to help others who ache?

6. Read Psalm 145:18–19. In what specific ways has Jesus been alert and responsive to you lately?

11

Recapturing the Real Jesus

Our Savior Is *Wildly* Faithful and *Wildly* Fearsome

It is madness to wear ladies' straw hats and velvet hats
to church; we should all be wearing crash helmets.

—ANNIE DILLARD

■ ■ ■ ■ ■ ■

Several years ago during Christmastime, my dear friend Eva (Judge Andrew's even-better half!) had a memorable moment with her very dissimilar little girls, Abby and Audrey. Abby is a responsible, well-mannered young lady. Audrey came out of the womb kicking and hasn't really stopped. Eva often says, "If Audrey had been born first, there wouldn't be an Abby!"

On that particular December morning when the girls were six and two and a half respectively, Abby was carefully helping Eva drape a garland around the piano while keeping a wary eye on her rambunctious baby sister. Abby had cause for concern because Audrey had recently begun showing a keen interest in the porcelain baby Jesus that served as the centerpiece of their living room nativity set. Much to Abby's chagrin, "Jesus" had disappeared from the scene several times, only to reappear a few hours later with a smudge of grape jelly or the conspicuous shimmer of saliva.

Sensing the tension building between her daughters, Eva glanced over and noticed that, indeed, Audrey's behavior seemed suspicious. She was wearing a mischievous grin and had her hands buried in her armpits as if she was hiding something. Suddenly she spun around and took off down the hall, a gleeful cackle echoing behind her. Abby wailed, "Mama, I think she's got baby Jesus!"

Eva replied, "Well, honey, I'm all tangled up in this garland, so you'll have to go find Him." Which sent Abby tearing off in the direction Audrey had just disappeared. Within seconds Eva heard the high-pitched sounds of scuffling girls—not unlike alley cats—several rooms away. She said she fully expected her eldest to return with a shattered ceramic Savior. Instead, a few minutes later Abby came merrily skipping back and announced, "Don't worry, Mom. It was only Joseph!"

> Have you ever felt as if Jesus was *missing*—
> that He wasn't where you expected Him to be?

I can so identify with Abby. For the past several years, I've been on a passionate quest to find my hijacked Prince. To lay claim to the *real* Jesus. To discover the entirety—as best I can with a finite human mind—of Immanuel. I won't accept a watered-down caricature anymore. I want to know the profoundly compassionate Lord who wept when His friend Lazarus died…the very same One who filled the temple with terrifying glory.

Nothing less than the *wildly faithful* Lamb who was slain and the *wildly fearsome* Lion of Judah will keep my heart captive!

THE DIVINE DICHOTOMY OF SAFE AND STRONG

Individually speaking, the terms *lion* and *lamb* are simply metaphors. Only when they're considered in tandem do these descriptors become a relatively accurate depiction of Christ's character. Jesus is both perfectly awe-inspiring and perfectly accessible. He is the Lion of Judah who tears the wicked to pieces, and He is the Lamb who was slain for our sins.[1] He's the King of kings who deserves our complete obeisance and reverence, yet He is so loving we can launch ourselves into His lap with the assurance that He'll catch us and hold on.

▪ ▪ ▪ ▪ ▪ ▪ The *Wild* Ways of God ▪ ▪ ▪ ▪ ▪ ▪

Obviously, God doesn't have two eyes, two feet, or ten fingers. He's not restricted by a physical form like a human. So when I talk about "launching ourselves into Jesus's lap" or when King David wrote, "When I look at your heavens, the work of your fingers" in Psalm 8, we're using anthropomorphisms to describe God from a human perspective. The word *anthropomorphic* means "ascribing human form or attributes to a being or thing not human, especially to a deity."[2] However, when Jesus walked this earth in a suit of skin, He *did* have human form and attributes.

This divine dichotomy is admittedly mystifying. Author and theologian J. I. Packer wrote about the reluctance we have to recognize the existence of mystery and to let God be wiser than men.[3] Yet divine concepts will always exist beyond human comprehension, and frankly, subjecting our Savior to human logic is kind of like trying to study an elephant with a PlaySkool microscope!

Fortunately, there are many scriptural illustrations that help elucidate the duality of Jesus. Two of my favorites involve the disciple John. Now I have to be honest and admit that John wasn't on my original top-ten apostles list because he refers to himself as "the one Jesus loved," not once, not twice, but *five times* in the gospel of John.[4] I thought he was a bit of a braggart. I could totally picture the other eleven guys exchanging sideways glances and rolling their eyes when he started up with the *I'm-so-loved* exclamations! But the more I perused his life story, the more apparent it became that John wasn't an attention-seeking teacher's pet; he was simply a man so dramatically transformed by the love of Christ that he couldn't help but talk about it every time he opened his mouth or picked up a pen.

In this first scene illustrating the approachable side of our Savior, John was hanging out with Jesus at the last Passover meal they would eat together when he leaned in to ask who the betrayer would be:

> After saying these things, Jesus was troubled in his spirit, and testified, "Truly, truly, I say to you, one of you will betray me." The disciples looked at one another, uncertain of whom he spoke. One of his disciples, whom Jesus loved, was reclining at table close to Jesus, so Simon Peter motioned to him to ask Jesus of whom he was speaking. So that disciple, leaning back against Jesus, said to him, "Lord, who is it?" *John 13:21–25*

Now that's what I call close! John had such an intimate relationship with Jesus he was able to recline against Him. He literally felt the rise and fall of Immanuel's breast. The God who holds the moon and the stars in His mighty right hand held John. It's no wonder he referred back to that affectionate embrace fifty years later as he composed his gospel near the end of his life, long after the "leaning" event actually happened:

> Peter turned and saw that the follower Jesus loved was walk-
> ing behind them. (This was the follower who had leaned
> against Jesus at the supper and had said, "Lord, who will turn
> against you?") *John 21:20, NCV*

Much had happened in John's life since that symbolic supper when he'd been a naive teenager. He'd been heartbroken by his Lord's death on the cross. Then only a few days later, he felt his heart leap within his chest when Peter told him Christ had risen from the dead! Shortly thereafter he was dumbstruck when the tornado-like wind that blew threw the disciples' Pentecost party turned out to be the Holy Spirit. In the decades that followed, John preached, planted churches, and watched a paralytic turn cartwheels because of the healing power of Jesus's name. He also

■ ■ ■ ■ ■ ■ ■ ■ **Did You Know...** ■ ■ ■ ■ ■ ■ ■ ■

Most conservative Bible scholars believe the gospel of John was written by the apostle John sometime in the thirty years before his death in AD 100. Two key factors in determining the date of origin are the references to the "Sea of Tiberias" in John 6:1 and 21:1, which was a name widely used for the Sea of Galilee in the late first century, as well as the noticeable lack of references to the Sadducees (a Jewish political party), who ceased to exist after AD 70.[5]

suffered jail time, beatings, and homelessness as a result of his faith in the resurrected Messiah. But he didn't use any of those dramatic events to define himself when he penned his gospel account during the twilight of his life; instead, he described himself as the guy who leaned against the Lamb.

I'm committed to being defined by the embrace of Christ too. To be so indelibly marked by His affection that nothing can threaten my sense of belonging to God. For what it's worth, I've discovered that literally sinking into a pile of warm towels fresh from the dryer and closing my eyes while asking Jesus to hold me is a great way to practice the leaning thing!

The last book of the Bible describes an altogether different encounter John had with Jesus:

> Then I turned to see the voice that was speaking to me, and
> on turning I saw seven golden lampstands, and in the midst
> of the lampstands one like a son of man, clothed with a long
> robe and with a golden sash around his chest. The hairs of his
> head were white, like white wool, like snow. His eyes were
> like a flame of fire, his feet were like burnished bronze, refined
> in a furnace, and his voice was like the roar of many waters.
> In his right hand he held seven stars, from his mouth came a
> sharp two-edged sword, and his face was like the sun shining
> in full strength.
>
> When I saw him, I fell at his feet as though dead. But
> he laid his right hand on me, saying, "Fear not, I am the
> first and the last, and the living one. I died, and behold I am
> alive forevermore, and I have the keys of Death and Hades."
> *Revelation 1:12–18*

John didn't get all touchy-feely with Jesus here; instead, he collapsed to the floor in a dead faint. Seeing the Messiah in all His supernatural glory was simply too much for John's mental hard drive to process, and it crashed! He was undone by the fearsome majesty of God's only Son.

THE SWEETEST SURRENDER

My dear friend Cheryl Green recently told me a story about a missionary friend of hers named Greg, who is the president of Pioneer Bible Translators and who, along with his wife, spends most of his time in West Africa translating the Bible into a local dialect. She said even when Greg comes home to San Antonio on furlough, you can usually find him working away in the Oak Hills Church library.

A few years ago Cheryl, who volunteers in the women's ministry at their church, was walking down the hallway past the plate-glass windows of the library, and she looked in to see Greg sitting at a table by himself, weeping. She stepped inside to make sure he was all right and to ask if she could do anything to help. Greg responded, "Oh, I'll be okay, Cheryl. It's just that I'm translating the crucifixion."

We all should be so moved by what happened that very first Good Friday:

And the soldiers led him away inside the palace (that is, the
governor's headquarters), and they called together the whole
battalion. And they clothed him in a purple cloak, and twisting
together a crown of thorns, they put it on him. And they began
to salute him, "Hail, King of the Jews!" And they were striking
his head with a reed and spitting on him and kneeling down in
homage to him. And when they had mocked him, they

179

stripped him of the purple cloak and put his own clothes on him. And they led him out to crucify him. *Mark 15:16–20*

Roman soldiers jammed a wreath of thorns on our Savior's head to mock His claim of being a king. They wrapped His bleeding body in a violet robe, symbolizing royalty, to ridicule Him. They also hit Him and spit on Him. And all this took place *after* Jesus had been scourged, which meant He'd already been tied to a post and beaten with a leather whip interwoven with pieces of bone and metal that tore through His skin, probably exposing muscle and bone.[6]

It's a wonder the Lion of Judah submitted to such a severe beating. He could've let out a roar and ripped His assailants to pieces if He had wanted to. Instead, He humbly remained the Passover Lamb and staggered up a hill to His own slaughter. The King of kings allowed mean-spirited strangers to pound nails into His wrists and suspend Him on a tree between two common criminals. He condescended to a cruel and humiliating death. Yet even a casual observer to His crucifixion—a man who had no former relationship with Jesus—recognized the horror and drama as supernatural:

And Jesus uttered a loud cry and breathed his last. And the curtain of the temple was torn in two, from top to bottom. And when the centurion, who stood facing him, saw that in this way he breathed his last, he said, "Truly this man was the Son of God!" *Mark 15:37–39*

Three days later Jesus's resurrection verified His divinity.[7] The same tender Lamb with whom John shared a meaningful hug prior to the Cross was also the terrifying Lion who came roaring back to life, bellowing a battle cry and ripping the keys of hell and death from Satan's grimy hand.

Now that's *wild*. That kind of merciful and marauding Redeemer will rock your world!

■ ■ ■ ■ ■ ■ ■ The *Wild* Ways of God ■ ■ ■ ■ ■ ■ ■

Roman soldiers often broke the legs of whoever was being crucified to speed up the process of death by limiting their ability to push themselves up to breathe. The fact that they *didn't* break Jesus's legs and instead pierced Him with a spear[8] is yet another Messianic prophecy fulfilled by our Redeemer—"He keeps all his bones; not one of them is broken" (Psalm 34:20). Even during His physical death, before Christ's resurrection, God was in control!

TO LOVE AND RESPECT

There's only been one brief time period in my adult life when I felt petite, and that was when I dated a professional football player. He stood six feet six, and although he weighed almost three hundred pounds, he didn't have an ounce of fat on him. In fact, he looked as if he'd been chiseled out of granite, like some oversized statue of Adonis! When we walked down the street or into a restaurant together, I felt like a tiny feminine wisp of a woman. Frankly, being so small by comparison was a delightful contrast to the long list of men I've dated whose jeans probably wouldn't fit one of my thighs! It was a treat to be romanced by a guy whose biceps bulged when he tossed opposing players to the ground. But the magic died when his wimpy emotional capacity revealed itself and ruined the fairy tale.

Prior to the padded-pants-wearing Adonis, I dated a financial planner, one of the kindest men I've ever known. No matter what I said or how I behaved, he responded softly. At first I was drawn to his mild-mannered personality. I mused, *This guy would never abuse his wife or children, because he couldn't hurt a fly!* But one morning when we were driving toward the mountains for a day of skiing, I saw another side to his pacifism. He was cruising up the interstate at the posted speed limit when another driver pulled his Jeep beside us and gestured menacingly with his middle finger. For several horrible seconds our cars were barreling neck and neck down an icy stretch of cement. But then my guy panicked and, raising a hand in surrender, slammed on the brakes and veered across several lanes of traffic to get away from the Cherokee-driving lunatic. After narrowly avoiding an accident, he looked at me with an anxious expression and shrugged his shoulders pitifully. When I looked away, embarrassed for him, I noticed his hands were trembling so violently he was having a hard time hanging on to the steering wheel.

The handsome brute lacked heart, and Mr. Meek lacked gumption. Therefore neither one captured both my respect *and* affection, and neither relationship proved secure enough to last a lifetime. In stark contrast our Savior's beautiful blend of toughness and tenderness makes Him the *perfect* Bridegroom. (Marriage is often used as a metaphor to illustrate the kind of intimate relationship we can enjoy with Jesus.[9])

I'm especially aware and appreciative of our divine Husband's duality when I'm awakened by strange sounds in the middle of the night. Since I live out in the country and have had a few problems with a creepy neighbor, nocturnal noises sometimes jerk me into sudden consciousness.

My eyes frantically try to adjust to the dark, and my heart starts galloping in my chest. But then I'll take a few deep breaths and focus on what
a fierce warrior Jesus is, and my eyelids get heavy once more, my heart
returns to its regular rhythm, and I settle back to sleep in His figurative
arms.

In his classic book *Lion and Lamb,* Brennan Manning sums up Jesus's
amazing blend of ferocity and tenderness with a poignant story about a
man who peacefully fell into an even deeper sleep:

> The Lion and the Shepherd are one and the same. Ferocious
> pursuit and unwavering compassion are dual facets of the
> tremendous Lover who knows not only what hurts us but also
> how to heal us. And this savage and soothing God is also the
> Lamb who suffered the pains of death on our behalf. This was
> the experience of an old man who lay dying. When the priest
> came to anoint him, he noticed an empty chair at the man's
> bedside and asked him who had just been visiting. The sick
> man replied, "I place Jesus on that chair and I talk to Him."
> For years, he told the priest, he had found it extremely diffi-
> cult to pray until a friend explained that prayer was just a
> matter of talking with Jesus. The friend suggested he imagine
> Jesus sitting in a chair where he could speak with Him and
> listen to what He said in reply. "I have had no trouble praying
> ever since."…
>
> Some days later, the daughter of this man came to the
> parish house to inform the priest that her father had just
> died. She said, "Because he seemed so content, I left him
> alone for a couple of hours. When I got back to the room,
> I found him dead. I noticed a strange thing, though: his

head was resting not on the bed but on an empty chair that was beside his bed."

The Lion who will kill all that separates us from Him; the Lamb who was killed to mend that separation—both are symbols and synonyms for Jesus. Relentlessness and tenderness; indivisible aspects of the Divine Reality.[10]

If Jesus was only safe, we'd only feel accepted. If Jesus was only strong, we'd only feel protected. The fact that our Savior provides both warmth and shelter is what enables us to find real rest for our souls.

We need an untamed *Savior because...*

only a *wildly faithful and wildly fearsome* Jesus can free us to lean confidently into His affection *and* fall reverently at His feet—which is real worship!

■ ■ Living and Loving with Abandon ■ ■

1. Describe the last time you figuratively leaned against Jesus and listened to His heartbeat. How did you feel when you were being "held" by Him?

2. Read Daniel 7:9 and Proverbs 16:31. Those verses clarify that the "white hair" adorning Christ's head in Revelation 1 isn't a sign of

age but of wisdom and the respect He is due. What three or four characteristics do you respect most about our Redeemer?

3. Read Ezekiel 1:24 and 43:2. Since "rushing waters" (NIV) is the same metaphor used to describe God's voice, what do you think Jesus's literal voice will sound like? What would you *prefer* His voice to sound like?

4. Read Matthew 17:1–8. How does John's first experience with a transfigured Jesus compare to his fainting episode in Revelation 1?

5. What anthropomorphic terms would you use to describe Jesus to an unbeliever—without using the words *lion* or *lamb*—so as to convey His combination of approachability and formidability?

6. Read Proverbs 18:10. How would you rewrite this truth in your own words?

12

The Great Emancipator

Our Savior Is Wildly Liberating

The similarity between real freedom and the freedom
experienced by many Christians is the difference
between the taxidermist and the veterinarian; while
you do get your dog back, one collects dust while the
other jumps, slobbers, and barks.

—STEVE BROWN

■ ■ ■ ■ ■

Several summers ago I spent a long weekend in Colorado Springs with my dear friend Judy (and her pork-loving husband, Tom). I was especially excited about being with their little girl, Katie. Because we live so far apart, I hadn't been able to hang out with Katie much before then, and Judy and Tom were quick to grant my wish to share some quality time alone with their two-and-a-half-year-old. They thrust a bag filled with her favorite toys into one of my hands and a car seat into the other and said, "Have fun. We'll see you later!"

Katie and I began our bonding adventure with a leisurely walk in the park, where I discovered her fascination with flowers. Actually she liked the weeds too. It didn't really matter what botanical genus the plants came from so long as they were blooming. We moved on to the playground, where I discovered Katie's spindly little arms and legs belied the suctioning strength of a giant squid. Once she'd connected with the lower rings of the monkey bars, it was all but impossible to peel her off! After a few hours I thought it'd be a great idea to take a trip to the frozen yogurt store since I'd worked up quite an appetite with all the gardening and hovering.

I carried Katie into TCBY on my hip and watched her expression turn serious as I pointed out all the flavors and toppings she could choose from. After several long minutes of deliberation, I finally talked her into the soft-serve peach with a liberal showering of sprinkles. I couldn't help but smugly suppose, *Her mom will be pleased about the fruit part*, since Judy's a bona fide health nut who sometimes teases me about my questionable snack choices. After I paid and handed Katie her cup, she slowly dipped a white plastic spoon into the mountain of pink confection dotted with all the colors of the rainbow and daintily lifted a sample to her mouth. Then her eyebrows arched up, her eyes widened, her mouth split into a huge grin, and her head sort of lolled back on my shoulder. I'd never seen a child so enraptured by just one bite of frozen yogurt. I thought, *Wow, that's the best two dollars I've spent in a long time!*

When we pulled into the driveway and Judy walked out to find her baby girl in a sticky, happy daze, she anxiously informed me that Katie had never before eaten even a smidgen of processed sugar. No wonder she was euphoric! I'd just introduced her taste buds to the decadent glory of dessert.

> What are some sensory experiences—for example, eating dark chocolate, going for a long run, or kissing your husband—that cause you to feel euphoric?

The dreamy expression Katie wore in that yogurt shop came to mind recently when I was trying to describe to a friend the newfound freedom God has given me. I explained how, beforehand, I hadn't fully realized my *lack* of freedom. Of course I knew that life wasn't perfect, that we live in a broken world marred by sin. And I understood the theological reality that my crooked little heart will be prone to wander until I'm reunited with our Creator in heaven. But I've been a Christian since I was seven—almost as long as I've been a survivor of childhood molestation—and have earnestly sought a close relationship with Jesus. So I just assumed the 80 percent or so of liberated soul I had was as good as it gets.

When I finally received Jesus's gift of total release from the shame, resentment, and condemnation that had stalked me for forty years, it was like being introduced to sugar for the first time. I was overwhelmed by the sweetness of our Redeemer's *wildly liberating* grace!

LIBERTY-STEALING LIE

In his book *A Scandalous Freedom*, author, pastor, seminary professor, and radio host Steve Brown describes the falsehood that keeps us distant from the freedom God offers:

> My father became a Christian three months before he died. His Christian physician said to him, "Mr. Brown, you have three months to live. Let's have a prayer, and then I want to tell you about something far more important than your cancer." That physician told my father about God's grace, about the cross, and about how the Christian faith was for sinners, including him. I will be eternally grateful for that man and his witness to my father.
>
> My father never went to church. Oh, he'd make a visit when my brother or I sang in the children's choir or did a recitation; but other than that, he stayed away. He never said bad things about church people. He never called them hypocrites or claimed they failed to live a life commensurate with

their confession. In fact, my father thought just the opposite. He honestly felt that those folks in the church were good people.

My father didn't go to church precisely because *he didn't feel he was good enough.*

That makes me angry. It makes me angry with myself and any others who—maybe even without meaning to—sent out the message that there were good people and bad people, and the good ones were in church. By our self-righteous attitudes, I, and a lot of other well-meaning people, discouraged my father from knowing Christ, rejoicing in Christ's redemption, and being free to live, laugh, and dance. In doing so, we violated the very essence of the gospel.[1]

His observations sure ring true in my world. When I've secretly wondered whether a woman in a low-cut shirt who reeked of cigarette smoke was good enough to join our Christian clique, I've desecrated the gospel. I sometimes forget it was *while I was still a sinner* that Jesus chose to give

The *Wild* Ways of God

When we fully recognize the forgiveness God gives us, we're enabled to forgive others.[2] As one biblical scholar has noted, "The greater righteousness Christ demands is not an entrance requirement to get into the kingdom but *a lifestyle characteristic that God enables those who come to him in Christ increasingly to approximate.*"[3]

up His life for me.[4] And to be completely honest, the minute I begin to notice others' unrighteousness is the moment my own is looming large. So I attempt, often subconsciously, to feign and dodge the Holy Spirit's conviction by pointing out their junk.

Clumsy efforts to distract God from noticing our mistakes would be humorous if they weren't so sad.

FISHING LESSONS

My tendency to notice the splinter in other people's eyes so as to avoid the lumberyard in my own is one of the reasons I identify with Peter, the disciple who angrily sliced off someone's ear to protest his betrayal of Jesus mere hours before Peter betrayed Jesus three times himself.[5]

But let's back up and start at the beginning of bumbling Pete's relationship with Jesus:

> One day as Jesus was preaching on the shore of the Sea of
> Galilee, great crowds pressed in on him to listen to the word
> of God. He noticed two empty boats at the water's edge, for
> the fishermen had left them and were washing their nets.
> Stepping into one of the boats, Jesus asked Simon, its owner,
> to push it out into the water. So he sat in the boat and taught
> the crowds from there. *Luke 5:1–3, NLT*

Like my stepfather, Peter was an avid angler. He probably kept a stack of fishing magazines in the bathroom and had lures littering his dashboard. Surely he'd sailed up to the shore of Galilee many times with a jaunty grin and a cooler full of fish. Of course, like frustrated fishermen the world over, he'd also idled up to the dock, grumpy and sunburned after a long day on the lake with no luck. The story Luke records in chapter 5 was one of those latter days. Pete and his buddies had fished all night yet still came up empty-handed. So he was probably glad when Jesus asked to use the prow of his boat as a pulpit; at least it'd serve some positive purpose!

I can picture Pete relaxing at the back of the boat with one long brown leg stretched out and his foot propped up on a bait bucket. Remember, he met Jesus through his little brother Andrew, who enthusiastically proclaimed Him to be the Messiah,[6] and that same belief had been slowly bubbling up in Peter ever since. He smiled as the boat swayed during Jesus's sermon, thinking about all the adventures he and Jesus and Andy had already shared. While he'd never had the patience for formal schooling, Peter pondered how much he was learning from this radical rabbi.

But then Jesus interrupted his thoughts and poked his pride:

When he had finished speaking, he said to Simon, "Now go out where it is deeper, and let down your nets to catch some fish."

"Master," Simon replied, "we worked hard all last night and didn't catch a thing." *Luke 5:4–5a, NLT*

You can almost hear the edge of exasperation in Peter's voice. Sure, he was beginning to believe Jesus was the Lamb of God and all that, but He was obviously a city boy, because everyone knew you wouldn't catch any fish in the heat of the day. Gruff Pete probably rolled his eyes at the other guys on board to further emphasize how dumb the command was before continuing with a hint of sarcasm:

"But if you say so, I'll let the nets down again." *Luke 5:5b, NLT*

Even the splash of the nets hitting the water wasn't loud enough to silence Peter's aggravated sigh. But moments later his aggravation morphed into amazement:

And this time their nets were so full of fish they began to tear! A shout for help brought their partners in the other boat, and soon both boats were filled with fish and on the verge of sinking.

When Simon Peter realized what had happened, he fell to his knees before Jesus and said, "Oh, Lord, please leave me—I'm too much of a sinner to be around you." For he was awestruck by the number of fish they had caught, as were the others with him. His partners, James and John, the sons of Zebedee, were also amazed. *Luke 5:6–10a, NLT*

After Peter realized how foolish he'd been to doubt Jesus, he fell at His feet and confessed his arrogance and his ignorance. But Jesus didn't give him a dirty look or issue a stern rebuke. He didn't even say, "I told you so." He just told him not to be afraid…and to prepare for a job change:

Jesus replied to Simon, "Don't be afraid! From now on you'll be fishing for people!" And as soon as they landed, they left everything and followed Jesus. *Luke 5:10b–11, NLT*

SAME SONG, DIFFERENT STORY

After their showdown on the water when he realized Jesus was God, Peter became a devoted disciple of Christ and followed Him wherever He went to teach, preach, and heal the sick. And that first fish story paled in comparison to the other miracles he witnessed Jesus perform. He watched his Master waltz on water in the middle of the night, assuming at first He was a ghost.[7] He saw a twinkle in the eye of Moses, who'd been physically dead for centuries, when he and Elijah appeared next to a supernaturally radiant Savior on the Mount of Transfiguration.[8] And he stared in shock when Jesus's friend Lazarus walked out of the grave, leaving a trail of burial rags behind him.[9]

Basically, Pete spent the better part of three years gaping at glory. Which is why you wouldn't think he, of all people, would stumble in his walk of faith. Yet Pete—whom Jesus affectionately called "the Rock"— slipped up so badly some wondered if he'd ever walk right again. And really, who would have blamed him if he'd ducked his head in shame for the rest of his life once everyone found out he'd been the coward who vehemently denied even knowing Jesus during His most difficult trial? How could he ever get past the guilt of running away while his Redeemer died a slow, painful death?

A few days after Christ hung on the cross, was buried in a borrowed tomb, and rose from death back to life, an overwhelmed and confused Peter decided to go fishing. He probably thought that being on the water would ease the tension in his head. That maybe sailing away from the incriminating stares would bring a modicum of peace. Some of the other disciples saw him loading the boat and said, "Hey, how about we join you?" Peter nodded yes with watery eyes, grateful for the company of friends who knew about his treachery yet hadn't abandoned him:

Later, Jesus appeared again to the disciples beside the Sea of Galilee. This is how it happened. Several of the disciples were there—Simon Peter, Thomas (nicknamed the Twin), Nathanael from Cana in Galilee, the sons of Zebedee, and two other disciples.

Simon Peter said, "I'm going fishing."

"We'll come, too," they all said. So they went out in the boat, but they caught nothing all night. *John 21:1–3, NLT*

I wonder what they talked about while the waves lapped at the sides of the boat that night. Maybe they discussed the details of the previous week in Jerusalem, wondering out loud if they could've done something to prevent Jesus's murder. Or maybe they were mostly quiet and contemplative, each man remembering private moments he'd shared with the Savior. But the following morning something so amazing happened they were compelled to talk about it for years afterward:

At dawn Jesus was standing on the beach, but the disciples couldn't see who he was. He called out, "Fellows, have you caught any fish?"

"No," they replied.

Then he said, "Throw out your net on the right-hand side of the boat, and you'll get some!" So they did, and they couldn't haul in the net because there were so many fish in it. *John 21:4–6, NLT*

John doesn't tell us that Peter was feeling a strong sense of déjà vu, but he had to be. They'd been out all night long on the very same lake where the first miraculous fish haul had happened and had returned home with empty ice chests. Yet, once again, the following morning they score an inexplicable, net-breaking catch. Surely bumbling Pete had goose bumps on his leathery skin as he squinted to get a better look at the man on the shore:

197

stead, this dear yet fantastically flawed man leaped into the lake and
began a freestyle sprint toward his Redeemer. Peter was so excited to re-
connect with his Savior he couldn't wait even the few minutes it would've
taken him to row to shore!

Humanly speaking, Peter should have been reeling with guilt. Instead, his race toward Jesus serves as a neon sign proclaiming God's mercy

■ ■ ■ ■ ■ ■ The *Wild* Ways of God ■ ■ ■ ■ ■ ■

Peter—the same guy who shot off his mouth and
whacked people with swords—matured into one of the
primary leaders of the early Christian church after the
death and resurrection of Jesus. His leadership is especially evident in the first half of Acts when the good
news spread like wildfire. Pete even paved the way for
Paul's missionary work with non-Jews when he visited
the home of Cornelius, a Gentile, and led him to Christ.[10]

198

for even the most notorious sinners. Jesus doesn't just forgive us; He fully restores our ability to interact with Him free of self-recrimination and regret. He liberates us from the unbearable load of shame.

LOSING THE LIMP

When I was a toddler, I was a rocker. Not the spandex-pants-and-electric-guitar kind, but the full-bodied-pitching-to-and-fro-on-my-hands-and-knees-in-the-crib kind. I used to rock so aggressively that Mom and Dad would be jolted awake by a loud *wham* when the crib completed its journey across the room and collided with the opposite wall!

Initially my parents weren't too concerned about my drywall-denting bedtime routine. At least I wasn't gobbling glue or sticking forks into electrical outlets. But then our pediatrician noticed I was pigeon-toed, and when x-rays revealed leg bones that resembled a set of parentheses, I was bundled off to an orthopedic specialist.

I liked going to his office at first because the doctor was nice and the nurse always gave me one of those lollipops with the loop handle, which were much tastier than the generic suckers they gave out at the bank. However, my enthusiasm faded when he prescribed leg braces for me to wear sixteen hours a day. The mandatory contraption buckled around my waist with a thick leather strap from which protruded heavy steel bars that extended down either side of my bowed legs all the way to my ankles. Except for a stubborn hinge near the knee, they were like full-leg casts, only squeakier. (Forrest Gump wore a similar style.)

I still remember tottering down the halls of Southside Elementary School like the Tin Man in *The Wizard of Oz.* The worst part was not being able to run or jump. I wasn't even allowed to participate in recess. It was sheer torture watching Charlene Williams boot home runs in kickball while I sat stiffly at the edge of the field with robot legs. Day after day after day throughout kindergarten and the beginning of first grade, my lower half was mostly immobilized in metal.

Then out of the blue one afternoon, the doctor said I could take them off. Just like that I could run and jump again. The very next day I beat Charlene Williams in the high jump contest. It was almost as if I had springs in my legs. I felt as though I could fly.

As a kid I was hobbled by an orthopedic device, but as a woman I've been hobbled by the scars of sexual abuse, the shame of my own sins, and a myopic view of the Messiah. Maybe, like me, you've also wobbled along as the result of molestation, mistakes, or misunderstanding. Thankfully our Savior came to set captives free. To liberate people from limping.

It may take a while to loosen up, but when sinners like us engage with the fullness of Christ—with His wildly redemptive, unsettling, tough, devoted, compelling, pro-women, confident, confrontational, unconventional, faithful, fearsome, and attentive nature—we become spiritually and emotionally emancipated! We start shimmying on God's dance floor! Plus He never gives up, even on desperately disabled followers like Pete and me. Our Creator is true to His Word:

So if the Son sets you free, you will be free indeed.
John 8:36, NIV

Mind you, we won't be *fixed*—that's not going to happen until God calls us home—but, hallelujah, we can be set *free*!

We need an untamed *Savior because...* only a *wildly liberating* Jesus can break the multiple chains that bind us!

▪ ▪ Living and Loving with Abandon ▪ ▪

1. If you had to score the percentage of your heart that's truly free, what would that number be?

2. What negative emotions tend to crop up over and over again in your life (for example, anxiety, insecurity, fear)?

3. Read Psalm 73. How do you resonate with the psalmist's lament about pagans prospering while God's children suffer? How can we as Christians reconcile the seeming lack of fairness in our world?

4. Read Galatians 5:13. What do you think Paul meant by the exhortation to "serve one another" in the context of freedom? How would you describe the relationship between spiritual liberty and authentic love?

5. In his book *A Scandalous Freedom,* Steve Brown writes, "What repeatedly kills our witness is pretense, not freedom."[11] What pretentious behavior in Christians do you think repels unbelievers the most, and what does that reveal about areas in our community that need the liberating touch of Jesus?

6. Read Romans 8:34 and Matthew 18:21–35. Is there any shame still festering in your heart because of sins you've already repented of? Any resentment over sins someone else committed against you? If so, what steps will you take today to seek freedom from those chains?

Notes

Introduction: Beauty on the Other Side of the Brink
1. Francis Chan, *Crazy Love: Overwhelmed by a Relentless God* (Colorado Springs, CO: David C. Cook, 2008), 20.

Chapter 1: Exposing the Myth of a Milquetoast Messiah
The epigraph to this chapter is taken from Dorothy Leigh Sayers, *Creed or Chaos?* (New York: Harcourt, Brace, 1949), 6.
1. Craig L. Blomberg, *Jesus and the Gospels: An Introduction and Survey* (Nashville: Broadman & Holman, 1997), 207–8; and *ESV Study Bible* (Wheaton, IL: Crossway Bibles, 2008), 1954.
2. See Deuteronomy 25:5–10.
3. See Genesis 19:17.
4. *ESV Study Bible*, 84.
5. See Deuteronomy 23:3.
6. See 2 Samuel 11:1–12:25.
7. Stephen M. Miller, *The Jesus of the Bible* (Uhrichsville, OH: Barbour, 2009), 35.

Chapter 2: The God Who Leaves Men Gaping
The epigraph to this chapter is taken from A. W. Tozer, *The Knowledge of the Holy* (New York: HarperCollins, 1961), 8.
1. See Exodus 23:14–17; 34:22–23; Deuteronomy 16:16.
2. William Hendriksen, *New Testament Commentary: Exposition of the Gospel According to Luke* (Grand Rapids: Baker Book House, 1996), 184.

3. Charles R. Swindoll, *Jesus: The Greatest Life of All* (Nashville: Thomas Nelson, 2008), 49.

4. Scotty Smith, "Spiritual Formation and Discipleship in a Post-modern Culture" (class lecture and syllabus notes, Covenant Theological Seminary, St. Louis, Missouri, January 16–April 24, 2006).

5. Swindoll, *Jesus,* 50.

6. Hendriksen, *Exposition of the Gospel According to Luke,* 186.

7. Swindoll, *Jesus,* 51.

8. Robert H. Stein, *The Method and Message of Jesus' Teachings* (Louisville, KY: Westminster John Knox, 1994), 4–5.

9. See Psalm 56:8.

10. See Psalm 34:18; Proverbs 18:10.

11. See Matthew 13:55–56.

12. See Mark 5:30–32; 13:32.

Chapter 3: The Very Best Friend of All

The epigraph to this chapter is taken from C. S. Lewis, *Letters of C. S. Lewis* (New York: Harcourt Brace Jovanovich, 1966), 231.

1. See Luke 1:5–25.

2. See Matthew 3:1–12. John's camel-coated appearance would've certainly reminded people of the prophet Elijah, who dressed the same way and preached a similar fiery message of repentance (2 Kings 1:8).

3. Gene Edwards, *The Prisoner in the Third Cell* (Wheaton, IL: Tyndale, 1991), 19–20.

4. See Malachi 3:1.

5. See 1 Peter 2:22.

6. Stephen M. Miller, *The Jesus of the Bible* (Uhrichsville, OH: Barbour, 2009), 105.
7. See 2 Kings 5.
8. See Luke 3:19–20.
9. *ESV Study Bible* (Wheaton, IL: Crossway Bibles, 2008), 1824.

Chapter 4: Rough, Tough, and Ready to Rumble

The epigraph to this chapter is taken from Susan R. Garrett, *The Temptations of Jesus in Mark's Gospel* (Grand Rapids: Eerdmans, 1998), 82.

1. *ESV Study Bible* (Wheaton, IL: Crossway Bibles, 2008), 1824.
2. See Luke 2:51–52.
3. See Matthew 13:55; Mark 6:3.
4. Edward W. Goodrick and John R. Kohlenberger III, eds., *Zondervan NIV Exhaustive Concordance* (Grand Rapids: Zondervan, 1999), 1596.
5. See 1 Kings 5:1–12.
6. Stephen M. Miller, *The Jesus of the Bible* (Uhrichsville, OH: Barbour, 2009), 87, and John Tiffany, "New Revelations on the Life of Jesus," *The Barnes Review.org*, www.barnesreview.org/html/nov2006lead.html.
7. Robert H. Stein, *Jesus the Messiah: A Survey of the Life of Christ* (Downers Grove, IL: InterVarsity, 1996), 105–6.
8. Mark Galli, *Jesus Mean and Wild: The Unexpected Love of an Untamable God* (Grand Rapids: Baker Books, 2006), 24.
9. See Matthew 4:8; 5:1; 17:1–13; 28:16–20.
10. See Romans 8:33–39.

Chapter 5: Simply Irresistible

The epigraph to this chapter is taken from Charles Spurgeon's sermon "Love to Jesus," volume 6, sermon 338, www .spurgeongems.org.

1. See John 1:35–41.
2. See Mark 2:1–12.
3. See Luke 5:1–11; Mark 3:17; John 1:40–42; John 6:1–7; John 21:2; John 1:45–51; Mark 2:13–14; Luke 5:27–28; John 20:24–25; John 14:1–7; Mark 15:40; Acts 1:13; John 14:22; Luke 6:15; John 6:70–71.
4. William Hendriksen, *New Testament Commentary: Exposition of the Gospel According to Mark* (Grand Rapids: Baker Book House, 1975), 124.
5. Spurgeon, "Love to Jesus," www.spurgeongems.org.

Chapter 6: A Little Pink in the Party

The epigraph to this chapter is taken from William Hendriksen, *New Testament Commentary: Exposition of the Gospel According to Luke* (Grand Rapids: Baker Book House, 1978), 43.

1. Sharon Tanenbaum and Ashley Tate, "Solutions: New Uses for Old Things," *Real Simple,* August 2009, 36; Sharon Tanenbaum and Ashley Tate, "Solutions: Summertime New Uses for Old Things," *Real Simple,* July 2009, 36.
2. Taken from John Ortberg's message, "Was Christianity Opposed to Women?" www.johnortberg.com.
3. Cooperative Baptist Fellowship, "Responding to the Da Vinci Code: An Outline Resource for Church Leaders," 12, www .thefellowship.info/documents/tdvc.pdf.

4. J. Julius Scott Jr., *Jewish Backgrounds of the New Testament* (Grand Rapids: Baker Books, 1995), 248–49.

5. See Judges 4:4–8, 17–24.

6. See Matthew 17:14–20; Mark 5:1–13; Luke 4:33–37.

7. Hendriksen, *Exposition of the Gospel According to Luke*, 419.

8. *ESV Study Bible* (Wheaton, IL: Crossway Bibles, 2008), 1967.

9. See Matthew 27:55–56; Mark 15:40; John 19:25.

10. See Matthew 27:61; Mark 15:47.

11. Taken from John Ortberg's message, "Was Christianity Opposed to Women?" www.johnortberg.com.

12. *ESV Study Bible*, 1967.

13. *The Becoming: Devotional Bible for Women* (Nashville: Thomas Nelson, 2006), 1112.

14. This story is often attributed to twentieth-century mystic G. I. Gurdjieff.

15. See Mark 6:14–29.

16. See Matthew 2.

17. Stuart Hample and Eric Marshall, *Children's Letters to God* (New York: Workman, 1991).

18. Edward W. Goodrick and John R. Kohlenberger III, eds., *Zondervan NIV Exhaustive Concordance* (Grand Rapids: Zondervan, 1999), 1463.

Chapter 7: Not Your Average Boy Next-Door

The epigraph to this chapter is taken from James D. Bratt, ed., *Abraham Kuyper: A Centennial Reader* (Grand Rapids: Eerdmans, 1998), 461.

1. Leigh Montville, *The Big Bam: The Life and Times of Babe Ruth* (New York: Random House, 2006), 161–64.

2. William Hendriksen, *New Testament Commentary: Exposition of the Gospel According to Luke* (Grand Rapids: Baker Book House, 1978), 255.

3. See John 3:16–17; J. Alec Motyer, *The Prophecy of Isaiah: An Introduction and Commentary* (Downers Grove, IL: InterVarsity, 1993), 499.

4. Os Guinness, *The Call: Finding and Fulfilling the Central Purpose of Your Life* (Nashville: W Publishing Group, 1998), 45.

5. See Isaiah 30:21.

Chapter 8: The Divine Trait of Stepping on Toes

The epigraph to this chapter is taken from Søren Kierkegaard, "The Offense," in *Provocations: Spiritual Writings of Kierkegaard*, comp. and ed., Charles E. Moore (Farmington, PA: Plough Publishing, 1999), 171.

1. See Matthew 13:53–58; Mark 3:21; John 7:3–5.

2. *The Westminster Confession of Faith* (Atlanta: The Committee for Christian Education and Publications, 1990), 8.

3. Richard J. Foster and James Bryan Smith, eds., *Devotional Classics: Selected Readings for Individuals and Groups* (New York: HarperCollins, 1993), 287.

4. Mark Galli, *Jesus Mean and Wild: The Unexpected Love of an Untamable God* (Grand Rapids: Baker Books, 2006), 60–61.

5. See Matthew 11:4–5; Mark 12:41–44; Luke 14:12–14.

6. Walter C. Kaiser Jr., Peter H. Davids, F. F. Bruce, Manfred T. Brauch, eds., *Hard Sayings of the Bible* (Downers Grove, IL: InterVarsity, 1996), 442.

7. See Jeremiah 8:13; Hosea 9:10, 16; Joel 1:7; Micah 4:3–4; Zechariah 3:10.

8. See 1 Kings 4:25.

9. Kaiser, *Hard Sayings of the Bible*, 425–26.

10. Marilyn Chandler McEntyre, "Furthermore: Nice Is Not the Point," *Christianity Today*, November 13, 2000, 104.

11. Lisa Whittle, "Become the Girlfriend You've Always Wanted to Have…," *Connection*, Summer 2009, 20.

Chapter 9: Refreshingly Radical

The epigraph to this chapter is taken from Frederick Buechner, *Listening to Your Life* (New York: HarperCollins, 1992), 95.

1. "Dusky Pygmy Rattlesnake," Jacksonville Zoo and Gardens, www.jacksonvillezoo.org/animals/reptiles/dusky_pygmy_rattlesnake/.

2. Spiros Zodhiates, ed., *Hebrew-Greek Key Word Study Bible, NIV Edition* (Chattanooga, TN: AMG, 1996), 2122.

3. W. E. Vine, Merrill F. Unger, and William White Jr., *Vine's Complete Expository Dictionary of Old and New Testament Words* (Nashville: Thomas Nelson, 1996), 316.

4. See Matthew 8:19–20; Luke 9:57–58.

5. Author unknown, "You May Be the Only Bible Some Will Ever Read!" www.muscleshoalsnazarene.org.

6. Francis Chan, *Crazy Love: Overwhelmed by a Relentless God* (Colorado Springs, CO: David C. Cook, 2008), 135–36, 150, 154–55.

7. See Matthew 11:19.

Chapter 10: Our Empathetic Hero

The epigraph to this chapter is taken from Henri Nouwen, *Jesus: A Gospel* (Maryknoll, NY: Orbis, 2001), 38.

1. Edward W. Goodrick and John R. Kohlenberger III, eds., *Zondervan NIV Exhaustive Concordance* (Grand Rapids: Zondervan, 1999), 1591.

2. Philip Yancey, *Where Is God When It Hurts?* (Grand Rapids: Zondervan, 1990), 23.

3. Ken Gire, *Moments with the Savior: A Devotional Life of Christ* (Grand Rapids: Zondervan, 1998), 110–11.

4. Ben Witherington III, *The Gospel of Mark: A Socio-Rhetorical Commentary* (Grand Rapids: Eerdmans, 2001), 102–3. See also Leviticus 13:45.

5. See Luke 4:40; Stephen M. Miller, *The Jesus of the Bible* (Uhrichsville, OH: Barbour, 2009), 143.

6. See Matthew 9:1–8; Mark 2:1–12; Luke 5:17–26.

7. See Matthew 8:13; 9:29; Mark 5:34; 6:5.

8. See Matthew 11:20.

9. Aleksandr Solzhenitsyn, *The Gulag Archipelago* (New York: HarperCollins, 2002), 312.

Chapter 11: Recapturing the Real Jesus

The epigraph to this chapter is taken from Annie Dillard, *Teaching a Stone to Talk: Expeditions and Encounters* (New York: HarperCollins, 1982), 52.

1. See Hosea 5:14–15; Revelation 5:12.

2. *Webster's Encyclopedic Unabridged Dictionary of the English Language* (San Diego: Thunder Bay, 2001), 88.

3. J. I. Packer, *Evangelism and the Sovereignty of God* (Downers Grove, IL: InterVarsity, 1961), 16.

4. See John 13:23; 19:26; 20:2; 21:7, 20.

5. Craig L. Blomberg, *Jesus and the Gospels: An Introduction and Survey* (Nashville: Broadman & Holman, 1997), 168–70; *ESV Study Bible* (Wheaton, IL: Crossway Bibles, 2008), 2015.

6. *ESV Study Bible,* 1885.

7. See John 20:1–18.

8. See John 19:33–34.

9. See Psalm 68:5; Song of Songs; Isaiah 54:5; Revelation 21:2.

10. Brennan Manning, *Lion and Lamb: The Relentless Tenderness of Jesus* (Old Tappan, NJ: Chosen Books, 1986), 129–30.

Chapter 12: The Great Emancipator

The epigraph to this chapter is taken from Steve Brown, *A Scandalous Freedom* (West Monroe, LA: Howard Publishing, 2004), 6.

1. Brown, *A Scandalous Freedom,* 136–37.

2. See Matthew 18:21–35; Luke 6:36.

3. Craig L. Blomberg, *Jesus and the Gospels: An Introduction and Survey* (Nashville: Broadman & Holman, 1997), 389.

4. See Romans 5:8.

5. See John 18:1–27.

6. See John 1:35–42.

7. See Matthew 14:22–33.

8. See Matthew 17:1–8.

9. See John 11:1–44.

10. See Acts 10.

11. Brown, *A Scandalous Freedom,* 12.

About the Author

Rarely are the terms *hilarious storyteller* and *theological scholar* used to describe the same person, but then, Lisa Harper is anything but stereotypical. She has been lauded as a gifted communicator whose writing and speaking overflow with colorful pop-culture references that connect the dots between the Bible era and modern life.

Best-selling author and pastor Max Lucado calls Lisa one of the "best Bible tour guides around," and speaker Priscilla Evans Shirer adds, "If anyone can help us to hear, understand, and receive the truth of Scripture, it is Lisa Harper."

Her vocational résumé includes six years as the director of Focus on the Family's national women's ministry, where she created the popular Renewing the Heart conferences, followed by six years as the women's ministry director at a large church in Nashville. Her academic résumé includes a Masters of Theological Studies with honors from Covenant Seminary in St. Louis.

Now a sought-after Bible teacher and speaker, Lisa is currently featured on the Women of Faith tour and also teaches at large multidenominational events and churches all over the world.

She's written nine books, including *Holding Out for a Hero: A New Spin on Hebrews* and *A Perfect Mess: Why You Don't Have to Worry About Being Good Enough for God.*

A Night of Real Christmas and **Coming Clean** are two unique inspirational events featuring Grammy-nominated artist Kim Hill and author and Bible teacher Lisa Harper. Both women are known for their humor, depth, and authenticity; their engaging style guarantees a program that will encourage everyone!

A Night of Real Christmas promises a special evening when women in your community will be transformed by the miracle that took place in a manger. Through worship, story, and biblical exposition, **Coming Clean** invites women into a transparent relationship with Jesus so they can truly flourish in God's incomparable affection. These events can be tailored to fit both ladies' night out and conference settings.

For more information on booking either of these events
for your church or ministry, please visit
www.lisaharper.net or www.kimhillmusic.com.